About Demos

Who we are

Demos is the think tank for everyday democracy. We believe everyone should be able to make personal choices in their daily lives that contribute to the common good. Our aim is to put this democratic idea into practice by working with organisations in ways that make them more effective and legitimate.

What we work on

We focus on six areas: public services; science and technology; cities and public space; people and communities; arts and culture; and global security.

Who we work with

Our partners include policy-makers, companies, public service providers and social entrepreneurs. Demos is not linked to any party but we work with politicians across political divides. Our international network – which extends across eastern Europe, Scandinavia, Australia, Brazil, India and China – provides a global perspective and enables us to work across borders.

How we work

Demos knows the importance of learning from experience. We test and improve our ideas in practice by working with people who can make change happen. Our collaborative approach means that our partners share in the creation and ownership of new ideas.

What we offer

We analyse social and political change, which we connect to innovation and learning in organisations. We help our partners show thought leadership and respond to emerging policy challenges.

How we communicate

As an independent voice, we can create debates that lead to real change. We use the media, public events, workshops and publications to communicate our ideas. All our books can be downloaded free from the Demos website.

www.demos.co.uk

First published in 2005
© Demos
Some rights reserved – see copyright licence for details

ISBN 1 84180 143 7
Copy edited by Julie Pickard
Typeset and produced by Land & Unwin, Towcester
Printed in the United Kingdom

For further information and
subscription details please contact:

Demos
Magdalen House
136 Tooley Street
London SE1 2TU

telephone: 0845 458 5949
email: hello@demos.co.uk
web: www.demos.co.uk

Start with People

How community organisations put citizens in the driving seat

Paul Skidmore
John Craig

DEMOS

Contents

Acknowledgements

We are very grateful to the Big Lottery Fund for supporting this research. Our thanks to Helen Thorne and Vanessa Potter, and in particular to Jill Wiltshire and Steve Browning who helped identify our case studies and offered invaluable advice and constructive criticism throughout the research.

We were very lucky to find such inspirational case studies, and such fantastically cooperative staff in all five willing to help us research their stories. Nicola Day at Just Ask Us, Paul Roberts and Jim Deery at the Ashton Centre, Lorna Langdon and Ann Brookman at Brumcan, and Laura McFadzen and Michelle Hegarty at Capability Scotland were generous in the time and energy they devoted to helping. At Envision, Tom Doust, Nick Nielson and Kate Wilcox made a very important contribution to the report, both through helping us to understand their work and by challenging and contributing to ours.

At Demos Verity Taylor, Kate Carey and Ian Craig helped to organise the logistics of our fieldwork and we were accompanied in Scotland by Paul Miller and in Belfast by Hannah Lownsbrough. Tom Bentley and Eddie Gibb made invaluable contributions in the writing of this report and Claire Ghoussoub, Abi Hewitt and Lisa Linklater all helped to make its publication and launch possible. We are very grateful to these and other people who will remain nameless, though any errors and omissions remain our own.

Finally we would like to dedicate this report to the Envisionaries we joined at Finsbury Park back in February last year. Through the enthusiasm and no-nonsense civic virtue they displayed that day they unwittingly set us on the intellectual journey which culminated in this pamphlet, and for that they have earned our sincere thanks.

Paul Skidmore
John Craig
May 2005

Foreword

Clive Booth

The creation of the Big Lottery Fund was the centrepiece of the Government's reforms of National Lottery Distribution announced in 2003. The Big Lottery Fund brings together the New Opportunities Fund (NOF) and the Community Fund, and will eventually take on the Millennium Commission's residuary responsibilities and ability to fund large-scale capital projects.

The Big Lottery Fund is a genuinely new body and our intention is to build on the best of all three organisations to create not only a bigger but a more intelligent funder.

This approach represents very good news for the voluntary and community sector, providing much more flexibility for us to respond to local circumstances and new ideas. There will be new opportunities for the sector to get involved at all levels. Between 60 per cent and 70 per cent of all our funding will still go directly to voluntary and community sector organisations. We will also put great emphasis on partnership working across sectors and on complementing national and local priorities and other funding streams.

At a time of considerable and exciting change it is also important for the Fund to reflect on what lottery funding has achieved for communities in the UK and what the priorities should be for the coming years.

This pamphlet has its origins in a study commissioned by the NOF in autumn 2003, before the merger but with an eye to some of the important questions a new body would need to be thinking about both during and after any merger.

This study had two aims. First, in uncovering evidence about the effects of participation, and whether involvement in community organisations like the ones we fund helps people to connect with wider society. Second, the processes at work in these organisations that make it possible for them to engage their users, members or citizens effectively. We also asked Demos to make recommendations about how lottery distribution bodies might best support community organisations in this work.

I think the Demos study provides some illuminating answers to those questions, and through the rich use of narrative and case study helps to bring home the importance of the work the community organisations we fund are doing in neighbourhoods across the UK.

The report makes a number of proposals for lottery and other funders which we welcome and look forward to exploring in more detail, and a number of which build on and take forward work we have already begun. We are particularly proud of our efforts to capture and promote good practice for all community organisations, and our work to support those we fund to reflect, learn and develop.

The report goes on to make a number of broader recommendations for government and other bodies based on the underlying principles the Demos team saw at work during their research. While it is obviously not the Fund's place to endorse these recommendations or comment on specific aspects of government policy, I hope these are valuable contributions to the ongoing debate about community empowerment and civil renewal.

Clive Booth is chair of the Big Lottery Fund

1. Start with people
The participation imperative

The art of association then becomes, as I have said before, the mother of action, studied and applied by all.

Alexis de Tocqueville, *Democracy in America*

Some corner of a muddy field

In an unremarkable corner of London's Finsbury Park, a 16-year-old girl hammers a wooden post into the ground as her friends look on approvingly. Nearby, another group uses rakes, picks and shovels to complete a shallow trench ready for paving stones to be laid. Others busy themselves building a raised flowerbed from wooden beams and piles of peat. In the thick of the action are Nick and Kate from Envision, a sustainable development charity that helps young people realise their capacity to make a difference.

As the hours pass and the weather turns ever more dismal, a certain order begins to emerge from the melee of people, tools and materials. The goal set at the beginning of the day – to build a community garden for people living in the area, the majority of whom do not have a garden of their own – suddenly begins to look more realistic.

While the weather may be typical for this time of year in London, the hive of activity in this corner of a muddy field seems anything but. It is the school holidays for one thing. Teenagers like these, we are led to believe, are more likely to be hanging around shopping centres or sitting at home watching TV than getting their hands dirty to help other people.

As it turns out, these young people did not just wake up this morning and spontaneously decide to be good citizens. Their commitment has been carefully nurtured. Before they could expect the 'Envisionaries', as the volunteers are called, to turn out on a rainy day in February, Envision needed to offer them an experience of civic participation that they would enjoy, and be prepared to repeat.

In fact the Envisionaries have many different accounts of the personal journeys that brought them here and what they have meant to them. Working in small groups in their schools across London over the last few months, they have conceived and carried out all kinds of distinctive and innovative practical projects. Some have installed solar panels and fair-trade vending machines in their schools. Others have concentrated on pressing local issues, such as a campaign to raise awareness about homelessness. One has even used his experience of the difficulties of growing up in inner-city London to set up an after-school club for young people at risk of getting mixed up in gangs.

The common thread running through their stories is about the experience of *getting involved*. Envision has given young people a channel through which to express their (often latent) desire to make a difference to their neighbourhoods or communities in ways which are meaningful and accessible to them, and which make it more likely they will want to do so again in the future. In the sense of fulfilment their projects have given them, the affinity with the organisation they have nurtured, and the sense of collective possibility they have created, Envision seems to have identified the ingredients of a potent recipe for nurturing engaged, involved citizens. And the secret of this recipe is something politicians are increasingly desperate to discover, as it becomes clear that there are limits to what government can deliver on behalf of citizens without their active engagement and involvement.

Our argument in this pamphlet is that, paradoxically, people will not be satisfied by what the public realm has to offer unless and until they become more active participants in shaping it. Improving the quality of the goods and services the public realm provides, like health and education, and reaffirming the values that underpin it, like trust, openness, solidarity and legitimacy, depends on finding ways to mobilise new forms of participation by citizens.

The challenge is to create 'communities of participation' which offer people the widest possible range of opportunities through which, and the widest possible range of settings in which, to play a more active role in shaping the decisions that affect their lives. If the renewal of the public realm increasingly depends on people's active participation within it, then we need to start with people: with the lives they lead, the values they hold, the relationships they care about and the interests that motivate them.

Community involvement has a recognised niche as a small but well established area of government policy. But in reality, whole swathes of public service reform depend on whether or not people can be engaged in this way. Policies to improve public health, reduce fear of crime and boost people's skills – now central to the promises of every major party – cannot succeed without the active involvement of millions of people. As our research shows, this involvement comes through practical relationships with certain kinds of organisation, not through some more abstract decision or form of communication.

The organisations, funding streams and methods set out in this report are fundamental to unlocking the full potential of public service reform. Mainstream providers like schools, hospitals and the police should learn important lessons from them. A new generation of policies is now promising 'choice' and 'personalisation' to citizens. The civic infrastructure we describe in this report, and the active citizenship it helps to foster, are essential to the realisation of that promise.

Equally critical, however, is that public policy should learn how community organisations – and smart ways to fund and support them – can help to create more demanding, intelligent users of mainstream services and to ensure that services are accessible and responsive to everyone, especially those who might not otherwise get to the front of the queue.

Public policy will have to learn how to strengthen support for this activity without co-opting it either into party politics or into the language and accountability structures of public service professionals. This creates new challenges and opportunities for the effective use of public funding streams such as those held by the lottery distributors. The report concludes with a series of independent recommendations designed to encourage greater innovation and effectiveness in the way that these questions are approached within government, among distributors of public money, and across the independent organisations which we believe can help to reshape and revitalise our experience of community life.

The work of Envision, like the other community organisations that have informed our thinking, suggests they are uniquely well placed to create new communities of participation because they have an ability to involve, engage and motivate people, which other types of institution find very difficult to emulate. Our aim has been to identify, in concrete detail, the organisational principles and practices on which this kind of ability is founded, so that government, funding bodies and other public agencies can do more to recognise, value and encourage it.

But we also seek to ask some more provocative questions about what the rest of society might learn from the most successful community organisations: to imagine a public realm whose institutions all understand the process of participation as deeply as they do, and to work through the sometimes radical implications for those institutions today.

Our conclusion is that politicians need to stop thinking of community organisations as resources that can be *used* as proxies for achieving the government's aims and instead respect them as partners with invaluable knowledge and experience to bring to the shared project of creating a more vibrant, participative public realm. That task today seems more urgent than it has for decades.

2. The decline of the public?

A century ago somewhere like Finsbury Park was a public space by virtue of who owned or built it. Parks have been the epitome of the public realm, where citizens have come together to play, perform, protest and party. Today, however, many parks are not public spaces at all, and do not invite participants. Publicly owned they may be, but many are unused, unsafe or in disrepair. In that sense, they provide a perfect metaphor for the 'decline of the public' that some people believe lies at the heart of modern society.

The story of this decay has been with us for decades, and has long been characterised in terms of a public spirit crowded out by private interests. Yet increasingly it seems that the threat comes less from invasions of the public realm than flights from it: people feel less and less willing, or less and less able, to believe in or act through established 'public' methods or institutions. This is expressed, for example, in growing distrust of government (see figure 1) and in the fact that while people are optimistic about the future in terms of their own lives, collectively we are pessimistic about the prospects for the future of society as a whole (see figure 2).

As disengagement and dissatisfaction have grown, the emphasis on reconnecting people with collective institutions has naturally grown. But for politicians of every stripe, and for New Labour in particular, this has been not just about their engagement with the formal institutions of government but about rekindling their attachment to

Figure 1 Growing distrust of government over time: percentage of those who trust the government always or mostly (1974–2003)

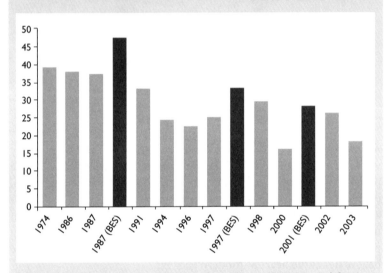

Source: British Election Study, University of Essex; see: www.essex.ac.uk/bes/ (accessed 17 May 2005).

some deeper notion of *community*. As Tony Blair said in a speech in 2000:

> *At the heart of my beliefs is the idea of community. I don't just mean the local villages, towns and cities in which we live. I mean that our fulfilment as individuals lies in a decent society of others. My argument . . . is that the renewal of community is the answer to the challenges of a changing world.*[1]

This reflects a growing consensus about the limits of states and markets alone in creating the conditions for a vibrant and prosperous society. Traditional demands on governments – for competent economic management, robust defence and security and the delivery

Figure 2 Hopes for future prospects: personal views compared with society as a whole

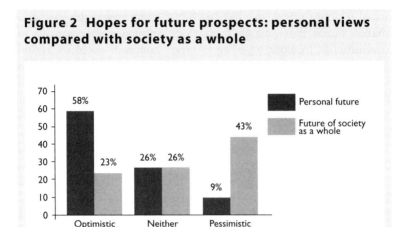

Source: Sociovision; see: www.sociovision.com (accessed 17 May 2005).

of public services – have not gone away, but they have been joined by a recognition that there is only so much that the state can accomplish from the top down, and that part of the challenge for government is to help communities help themselves: to support the individuals and organisations that sustain neighbourhood cohesion, to encourage engagement by citizens and to nurture the informal and organic processes and relationships that enable communities to tackle their own problems.

This analysis of the interdependence between formal governance and informal community participation sits within a current of thinking that goes back through Alexis de Tocqueville's famous admiration for civic association in nineteenth-century America to the civic republican tradition of Ancient Greece. However, its theoretical underpinning is the 'communitarian' agenda which emerged in the United States in the 1980s and 1990s, and particularly the growing body of research into the importance of 'social capital'.

Social capital is an appealingly simple proposition: the kinds of social relationships people have with one another, and the trust and shared values that emerge from them, influence the capacity of communities to work together to tackle common problems. Local government, schools, the police and other public institutions remain vital. But their impact is shaped and conditioned by the social capital of the communities they serve. To take an example, it is much easier to police a neighbourhood in which local people take it on themselves to identify and reprimand truancy, vandalism or other acts of anti-social behaviour, in which neighbours keep a vigilant eye on each other's homes and property, and in which people are prepared to report crimes and come forward as witnesses, than it is to police a neighbourhood in which fear, distrust or simply unfamiliarity preclude any of that from happening. Indeed, evidence suggests that the links between social capital and a wide range of social outcomes experienced by communities are powerful. 'Controlling for other key variables', writes Michael Woolcock, 'the well-connected are more likely to be housed, healthy, hired and happy.'[2]

Much of the credit for injecting such a motivating idea into the debate must go to the Harvard academic Robert Putnam. His analysis of declining social capital in the United States, captured in the metaphor of Americans 'bowling alone' rather than joining the bowling leagues that were popular in earlier decades, is hotly disputed inside the academy and out.[3] But it has resonated with policy-makers on both sides of the Atlantic. When the prevailing mood is more questioning of the potential for markets alone to create the conditions for a prosperous and vibrant society, and more suspicious of the limits and legitimacy of traditional state intervention, social capital offers a vocabulary for the times: emphasising common needs and responsibilities, while respecting the potential for individuals and their communities to address them without the heavy hand of the state. It is a political idea for an anti-political age.

Participation: the politician's dilemma

Despite the enthusiasm for Putnam's ideas, understanding how to translate them into a meaningful policy agenda has proved more difficult than expected. Putnam himself occasionally seems guilty of clinging to a rather nostalgic vision of how participation can be mobilised, recalling a bygone age of neighbourliness, altruism and civic virtue. One report concluded with '100 things you can do to build social capital', a list which included:

- attend town meetings
- say thanks to public servants
- sing in a choir
- get involved with Brownies or Cub/Boy/Girl Scouts
- if you grow tomatoes, plant extra for a lonely elder who lives nearby
- don't gossip.[4]

The call for a restoration of civic virtue to its proper place in people's lives may be impassioned, but this new traditionalism also feels rather implausible as the basis for genuine, far-reaching renewal.

This perhaps points to a deeper dilemma for politicians. Participation is more and more important to everything that they do, but it is not in their gift to engineer it. Instead they need to find ways to nurture social capital while staying out of the way of its 'natural', informal development.

At present, three answers about how to resolve this dilemma appear to be on offer. Each emphasises a different kind of citizenship, but none provides a very convincing account of how it can be mobilised.

The first account views citizens as *modernisers*. Citizens should be able to engage with collective institutions more on their own terms, by extending consumer choice to the users of public services like schools, hospitals and social care about what services they receive, how they receive them, and from whom. According to Alan Milburn, one of the most prominent advocates of this view:

The overall presumption should be towards a more diverse, more devolved, more flexible system of governance. It should be towards more choice for users. It should no longer be about central government acting as the proxy for the choices of local communities but for local communities themselves to be empowered to make those choices.[5]

Although choice sits at the heart of this analysis, the prescriptions that flow from it are largely structural. They include a call for a 'new localism' which transforms the relationship between government and frontline service provision, giving local services more autonomy from central control. There is also a presumption in favour of involving private and voluntary or community organisations where possible in the provision of public services on the basis that such diversity increases choice for users and keeps all providers on their toes.

The second account views citizens as *defenders*. Decades of privatisation and relentless obedience to consumerist impulses have threatened the professional and institutional cultures, rules and behaviours that the public realm is founded on. According to David Marquand:

the Victorians invented the public domain. Now it has to be reinvented. Its boundaries will have to be re-established, and they will have to be equipped with new barriers against incursions from the private and market domains.[6]

Public institutions and professionals like the BBC, civil servants and teachers should be freed of the burden of central control. New, more distributed centres of power and debate must be nurtured so that people will once again see the merit in citizenship and service, and be prepared to defend the public realm more vigorously from incursions by either the market or central government.

The third account views citizens as *agents*. Drawing inspiration from evidence that measures of social capital and levels of informal civic activity like volunteering have held up reasonably well in Britain,[7] this account tends to view local communities as an untapped resource that can be leveraged to make local services and initiatives more effective, responsive and legitimate. As one Home Office report puts it:

> A key reason for pursuing civil renewal is that local communities are just better at dealing with their own problems. They have the networks, the knowledge, the sense of what is actually possible, and the ability to make solutions stick.[8]

The challenge here is to breed a culture of 'active citizenship' in which 'citizens [take] opportunities to become actively involved in defining and tackling the problems of their communities and improving their quality of life'.[9] This culture change partly requires a new openness from institutions, hence the new emphasis on consultation and involving local communities in the governance of everything from schools to hospitals to regeneration partnerships to police forces. But it is also about changing the behaviour of individuals, helping them to learn the habits of good citizenship, for example through citizenship education, support for community organisations through new funding streams like the Big Lottery Fund, and initiatives to support volunteering like the Millennium Volunteers scheme and the Experience Corps.

Participation as an end in itself

The problem with all of these approaches is that they presume the purposes and boundaries of the public realm to be fixed and self-evident, and treat participation simply as a means to achieving these purposes or re-establishing these boundaries. The trick is to convince people that they want to participate, without pausing to really ask why or how they should. They seek to renew the public realm without thinking about the kind of 'public' lives that will animate it.

In this regard community organisations may be useful as proxies, with certain qualities that make them suited to doing this work on the government's behalf. But there is little discussion of what else they might have to offer.

Our argument in this pamphlet is that to treat participation as a means to an end in this way – as simply an expression of the potential for local people to refresh the parts of the public realm which the state cannot reach – sets up such a policy to fail, or at the very least to fail to reach its potential. That's because it overlooks the single most important lesson community organisations have to teach us about how such participation can actually be mobilised and channelled.

The most successful community organisations start with the people with whom they work. They revitalise the public realm not by walling it off or opening it up, but by bringing it to life: helping to connect it to people's lives, to make it meaningful to them, and in the process empowering them to reshape it for themselves. They function as *civic intermediaries* not by working to a set of predefined purposes but by contributing to communities of participation, in which citizens have the knowledge, capacity, confidence and motivation to act in whichever public or semi-public spaces and in whatever ways have most meaning for them – whether that means a neighbourhood, a school, a primary care trust, their home or the local supermarket.

We believe that government has much to learn from the organisations whose stories illuminate this pamphlet. But if it wants to nurture communities of participation, it cannot just contract out the task. To succeed, community organisations must be backed by a government more open than ever before not only to the decisions communities make but to the ideas they generate about what counts as 'the public realm', where it can be found, how it functions and what it is for.

To this end, we make two sets of recommendations. The first set refers specifically to the work of funders of community organisations, and in particular to lottery funders such as the Big Lottery Fund (set out below and discussed in detail in chapter 8). The second set applies to the public realm and the environments in which community organisations operate (set out below and discussed in chapter 9).

For funders of community organisations we recommend that:

1. Government and funders themselves must make a strong
    public case for funders' independent status. The two need
    to work together to forge a simple, sustainable public
    agreement about the position of lottery funders, creating
    the freedom to break new ground without the danger of
    them drifting off course.
2. All staff of lottery funders should spend at least one week
    a year 'on site' visiting and working in projects and
    organisations that their fund has supported.
3. Lottery funders should seek to make the process of
    reaching judgements about applicant organisations more
    open and effective, exploring the roles that can be played
    by the public and by other trusted local organisations.
4. Lottery funders should be given a duty to experiment, as a
    corollary of the special position that they hold. For
    example, lottery funders might seek to match local
    fundraising efforts to reward popular participation, to
    create an open source citizenship curriculum to develop
    and draw together knowledge about participation or to
    harness the intelligence of local professionals in fast-
    tracking funding to areas of greatest opportunity.
5. Funders should do more to develop their role as pro-
    active supporters of community organisations. They
    might seek to do this by brokering procurement
    relationships or networking community organisations
    together to share administrative capacity. One powerful
    example might be to create space for community
    organisations themselves in the Big Lottery Fund's new
    location. In this supportive role, lottery funders may
    increasingly be able to give voice to community
    organisations, helping them to share their knowledge
    more widely.
6. Lottery funders should make public not only their
    dependence on the hopes of individual players but their
    activism in fostering collective hope through their

support for community organisations. One way to do this would be to work with communities, local government, other funding agencies, the Office for National Statistics and the Audit Commission to create a national Social Hope Index.

7. Funders should explore the possibility of developing a 'trust first' approach, enabling the organisations that they fund to change the uses they make of funding in the event of a serious and unforeseen change in local needs and circumstances. Lottery funders should play a leadership role in establishing this approach as good practice.

In the final chapter, we build on this first set of recommendations, raising a wider set of questions about the environment within which community organisations operate. We seek to understand how this environment can enable the public to play a freer and fuller role in the public realm by exploring two areas:

O   public institutions as civic intermediaries
O   democratic representation and local governance.

First, we argue that this can happen only if we enhance the role that public institutions play as *civic intermediaries*. As a general principle, we argue that public bodies should help communities to make visible the collective possibilities they share and help to express their collective choices in ways that are meaningful to them. The suggestion is that faith in collective action is a key area for collective investment.

We suggest that across the voluntary and community sectors audit and inspection regimes should pay explicit attention to the way that public agencies contribute to and draw from the time, resources and enthusiasm at the disposal of their users or members.

Our final suggestion for helping public institutions to become civic intermediaries is that local councils should invest in their front-of-house, turning those with whom citizens interact from gatekeepers into brokers. We recommend that councils should build New York-style 311 phone systems,[10] using open source data systems to allow community organisations to use the council as a central point from which to access and distribute information about their work.

As well as helping public institutions to become civic inter-mediaries, we argue that as a society we need to create greater value from the connections popular participation creates between public services, civil society and our structures of democratic representation. We need to learn how harnessing these cross-cutting connections can help both to integrate the public realm and to foster what we describe as 'communities of participation'. In particular, we focus on the role that *democratic representation and local governance* can play in creating this value.

We focus first of all on the ways in which community organisations connect to more formal decision-making structures. We recommend that if communities can demonstrate sufficient popular support they should be granted a right of initiative to propose a local intervention and require local authorities to bring forth a proposal and vote on it. We also recommend that government, local authorities and com-munity organisations initiate a series of experiments in participatory budgeting.

We recommend that community organisations ought to be able to work in partnership with local political parties in bidding for government or lottery funds, managed jointly by the Department for Constitutional Affairs and the Home Office. We suggest that this process would support innovative citizen engagement projects and foster local re-engagement with national politics through political parties.

Finally, we concentrate on the idea, largely accepted, that protest, as well as participation, is a sign of a healthy democracy. We confront the question of how, in this context, we can create the condition in which protest is possible – the conditions in which those who disagree with prevailing political sentiment can nevertheless be heard. While fostering protest is a difficult area and must be explored with care, there is one mechanism that side-steps many of the problems it presents: a lottery. We recommend that organisations seeking to mount a lawful protest should be able to enter a government lottery to receive small grants to support their cause. Pro-hunt campaigners would have the same chance as anti-war marchers, a local residents' group against the siting of a mobile phone mast the same chance as an environmentalist group. With this last recommendation we confront head on the question of the role governments, community organisations and others can play in fostering inclusion, participation and value creation, and this is the subject with which the following chapters are concerned.

3. Participation and the three pillars of the public realm

The combination of a traumatic childhood and a difficult marital breakdown took a serious toll on Martin's mental health. During middle age he developed schizophrenia, a chronic condition little understood by the public at large even though it affects up to one per cent of the British population.

Martin's schizophrenia required that he receive treatment from the NHS to help him deal with both multiple acute episodes and their residual effects. He also attended meetings of a local Mind group, and received fantastic emotional support from other members of the group and from the two mental health professionals that came to assist them. But like many in his position, he felt the stigma of asking for help.

However, Martin refused to see himself as a helpless victim. A man of many talents and lively character, he was determined to put something back. Yet neither of his existing institutional relationships – as a recipient of care from the NHS, and a member of the Mind group – seemed to give him the chance.

That changed when an organisation called Just Ask Us began attending his Mind group. The organisation was set up as a healthy-living centre under the New Opportunities Fund (now called the Big Lottery Fund), focusing on the social causes of ill health, in particular rural isolation and lack of information about available services. For Just Ask Us, building a relationship with the Mind group was a delicate process. They sought the consent of both the professionals and the members, waiting to be invited rather than just expecting to turn up. They then worked hard to build the trust that was a precondition for the group to be willing to talk openly not just about what they needed to have but about what they wanted to do, and about how Just Ask Us could help them do it.

In Martin's case, what he wanted and what Just Ask Us was able to provide was a set of connections that allowed him to put something back in a way that had not seemed possible before. They helped him put his knack for storytelling and his expert knowledge of the beautiful countryside around Chichester to good use, by leading groups of walkers from the local community who come together to overcome the effects of rural isolation. He is also a talented artist, and sells his work to those he meets and others who view it at local galleries. Rightly, he feels that he now gives as much to the 'system' as he takes out. This feeling is fundamental to his sense of self-worth and self-efficacy.

Crucially, Just Ask Us also helped to ensure that Martin's personal experiences and views of the services he received counted when it came to influencing the governance of those services. Through the involvement of a cross-section of local agencies and providers, the organisation has the ear of the local authority in a way that no one of them alone could hope to have, and the experience of users like Martin directly influences the advice it gives about how service provision might be reshaped.

The three pillars of the public realm

The approach Just Ask Us took was undeniably simple, but it holds the key to a much more profound insight into what participation can mean and how it should be mobilised. In particular, it shows that the right forms of civic participation carry the potential to act on and strengthen three 'pillars' of the public realm at once:

- O   governance and democratic representation
- O   voluntary action and civil society
- O   public services.

Figure 3 Participation and the three pillars of the public realm

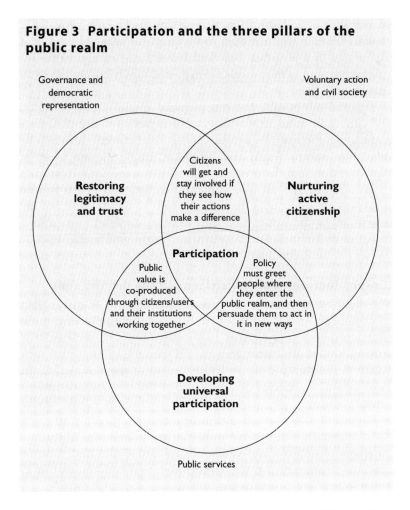

Governance and democratic representation

Voluntary action and civil society

Restoring legitimacy and trust

Citizens will get and stay involved if they see how their actions make a difference

Nurturing active citizenship

Participation

Public value is co-produced through citizens/users and their institutions working together

Policy must greet people where they enter the public realm, and then persuade them to act in it in new ways

Developing universal participation

Public services

Just Ask Us created an atmosphere in which Martin could be the kind of citizen he wanted to be, and a means by which his participation could simultaneously improve life for himself and others, and make formal institutions and governance structures more responsive. They did this by starting with what Martin wanted to get out of his participation – a desire to put something back. They provided a channel through which Martin could direct his personal needs and aspirations in a way that benefited himself and others within his community, and in the process strengthened the civic identities of all concerned.

This was only possible by being prepared to celebrate participation and citizenship as an activity that can be expressed in manifold ways and manifold settings, the precise connections between which may be difficult to discern. For Martin, being a schizophrenic and a user of public services and a keen walker and an artist are all-important parts of his life. But they are also important components of the way he practises citizenship, both the rights he feels he is entitled to and the responsibilities he feels it is his duty to bear. Just Ask Us was able to recognise and harness this in a way that conventional forms of public service provision could not.

'Co-production': putting citizens in the driving seat

The domestic agenda of New Labour's second term in government was dominated by debates about public service reform. Yet despite the efforts and resources directed to shoring up public services, it is striking how inadequately prepared the current model seems with regard to meeting the big policy challenges of the next decade. In 1997, Labour was elected on a platform of five key pledges based on simple, discrete interventions that government could make independent of other actors. Reducing class sizes, speeding up youth justice processes and cutting hospital waiting lists were all seen as questions of targeted applications of resources. The next wave of concerns, as prominent at the start of Labour's third term in office as in the second, appears much less conducive to such an approach:

O reconfiguring health and education systems to offer genuinely 'personalised' forms of provision
O building safer neighbourhoods
O tackling anti-social behaviour
O engaging citizens in the democratic process

○ providing appropriate social care for a growing older population
○ creating a full-scale childcare and early years infrastructure
○ the emergence of schools as 'full service' hubs for much wider forms of provision and engagement, particularly in deprived communities
○ increasing emphasis on health and well-being, particularly around tackling obesity, smoking and sedentary lifestyles.

These classically 'wicked issues' challenge traditional divisions of responsibilities and institutions along lines of function and historical role. They require many different stakeholders to work together to find solutions. Most importantly, as Bentley and Wilsdon argue, they place a much greater emphasis on citizens themselves:

Solutions rely, at least in part, on the users themselves, and their capacity to take shared responsibility for positive outcomes. In learning, health, work, and even parenting, positive outcomes arise from a combination of personal effort and wider social resources.[11]

In short, a new set of policy priorities is helping to move the participation of users in directly shaping services from the peripheral to a core concern. It is putting citizens in the driving seat.

At the heart of this analysis is the concept of 'co-production'. Co-production disrupts the view that responses to contemporary policy challenges like the ones we describe can simply be 'produced' by public services like schools, hospitals, the police or local councils. It offers an alternative framework for thinking about public goods which recognises explicitly the vital role that citizens themselves play in their creation. Citizens do not just receive these goods and services; they actively 'co-produce' them because their participation and behaviour are so important in determining the outcomes that are achieved. Environmental sustainability, for example, depends on how willing citizens are to use energy sparingly and recycle their waste; effective policing requires local communities to be vigilant and report crime; many health conditions could be prevented by changes in diet or lifestyle rather than treated with expensive drug treatments or surgical procedures.

Interest in co-production has coincided with a growing recognition that attempts to improve the performance of public services through the formula of 'investment and reform' will not by themselves yield significant improvements in prized social outcomes unless citizens can be persuaded to change the way they behave. In his landmark review of NHS financing over the coming decades, for example, Derek Wanless was categorical. The key factor determining which of his three cost projections ultimately comes to pass, he argued, is 'not the way in which the service responds over the next 20 years, but the way in which the public and patients do'.[12] A recent study of attempts by prisons to involve inmates in co-producing their rehabilitation found that those who had not taken part in education or training while in prison were three times more likely to be re-convicted than those who had.[13] In the experience of the Carnegie Trust, 'young people's solutions are both simpler and cheaper than our own and more effective because they own them'.[14]

But co-production is much more than a technical fix. It has a moral component that serves two important purposes. First, by breaking down the barriers between providers and users, co-production offers us a story about how citizens' personal interactions with collective institutions give them an opportunity to play a more active part in shaping the decisions that affect their lives. In this sense, it suggests a route to the historic ideal of liberty through self-government: the idea that the more individuals are able to participate in governing themselves, the greater their freedom. This may seem grandiose, but for Martin and thousands like him, the ability to reshape the services they receive is a hugely important form of empowerment.

Second, co-production reminds us that we are active contributors to a public realm that is also experienced by others around us. One familiar illustration of this is middle-class parents choosing schools that other middle-class parents choose, on the basis that their child's peer group will be important to their educational success. However, there are equally powerful examples across the public realm. In the context of public health, for example, preventing the spread of infectious or sexually transmitted diseases is contingent on individuals taking more responsibility for their own health and the health of others. Co-production promotes mutuality and empathy by inviting us to make the connection between our own individual moments of participation and interaction with collective institutions and the quality of the public realm experienced by others, and strengthens our sense of common citizenship.

The notion of co-production can draw together work to create an active citizenry and offers genuine prospects of success. Public agencies can use co-production as a yardstick for their broader contribution to the place in which they work. It serves as a timely reminder that the way in which local councils, for example, are able to deliver services, engage with citizens and work with intermediaries are tightly interconnected, and that strategic work can be done to improve all three. In Mark Moore's terminology, one way to create 'public value' is not only to find out what it is that the public values, but to help them to express it and to create it for themselves.[15]

Community organisations and co-production: breaking down the barriers

Why are community organisations well placed to enable co-production? One important reason is that they tend not to erect the same kinds of barriers between citizens and providers in the first place. Formal public services are hardwired with a bias towards the authority of professionals (doctors, teachers, police officers) over users (patients, learners, citizens). This is based on powerful and deeply held assumptions that the expert or codified knowledge of professionals is more valuable in the creation of positive social outcomes than the 'tacit knowledge' (what we sometimes think of as 'know-how', or the kind of knowledge, like the skill of riding a bike, which is difficult to put into words) of citizens and users. The classic statement of this view is Douglas Jay's observation that 'in the case of nutrition and health, just as in the case of education, the gentleman in Whitehall really does know better what is good for people than people know themselves'.[16]

The community sector is certainly not immune to these risks, particularly as organisations grow larger and more professionalised. But the organisations in our study showed that the sector at the very least retained a comparative advantage.

In its Vote 2003 project Capability Scotland, one of the largest disability organisations in Scotland, involved disabled people in every aspect of how it was run: several joined the steering group as equal partners alongside representatives from statutory bodies; others became spokespeople for the campaign by working with the media, information, news and dissemination panel; still others acted as agents provocateurs at their local polling stations.

The head of the nursery at the Ashton Centre in Belfast says that 'the kids play a big part in designing the summer scheme', ensuring not only that they enjoy it and are committed to attending, but that they learn to negotiate with one another. As a result of this participative approach, one of the parents of these children feels very confident about the care that they receive:

> If there are any problems, they will come and say, and it's not official , , , it's the informality.

> There's a more equal relationship, and they listen closely to the children.

The capacity for students to determine what projects they work on is also key to the appeal of Envision:

> It's not like [other initiatives] where you have to choose from what's on offer. We can do what we want.

> We get to choose what we want to do.

It's unstructured: we can do as much as we like.

You get to pick issues that matter to you.

You feel like you're independent.

Because they break down barriers facing users within their own organisation, community organisations are also well-positioned to act as brokers or intermediaries, helping people to navigate through the often complex and intimidating institutional landscape of formal public service provision to find the professional or service that meets their needs. Relationships between citizens and providers are not a given, nor are they distributed fairly. Disadvantaged or excluded groups may lack the knowledge or confidence to engage with providers in ways that other users just take for granted. We are all co-producers of public goods, but some co-produce more easily or effectively than others. However, the ability to engage with providers can be learnt and nurtured through careful support. This is where community organisations may have a unique part to play in enabling co-production to flourish. For many Just Ask Us users, co-producing their own health means finding a way to articulate their needs and concerns so that they can be met more effectively. But it also means feeling empowered to do so, and that is often the most important thing Just Ask Us engenders. As one person put it, 'They've taken the politics out of asking for help.'

Co-production: more is less or less is more?
Co-production is occasionally criticised for being an excuse to cut government spending, and for suppressing the power imbalances among different groups of citizens that would be affected by those cuts (it's easier to co-produce your own health if you can afford gym membership, personal training and a healthy diet). This has not been helped by the speed with which the political rhetoric that surrounds co-production has shifted into 'co-payment'.

Co-production does not necessarily mean public services doing more or less of what they have been doing. It is merely a way of thinking about existing approaches that draws attention to some of the most overlooked factors in their success or failure. By drawing attention to these factors, it becomes possible to identify interventions that are higher leverage, lower cost and more legitimate than reforms which focus only on public service institutions themselves.

Just Ask Us shows that often co-production is about discovering just how much *more* providers need to do. That's why the organisation has become very popular with providers of rural transport, whose buses they have helped to fill, while its relationship with social services, for whom new people mean an even heavier caseload, requires much more careful management. In fact, often everyone ends up working harder – Just Ask Us, local public service providers, and of course citizens themselves. But the results are that much more effective for it.

The power of trust

What makes this possible is an ability to cultivate deeper bonds of trust than traditional public institutions. The conventional model of legitimacy, rooted in faith in professional expertise and historic lines of accountability running from the individual institution through successive layers of governance to Whitehall and, ultimately, the Secretary of State, is widely seen to be teetering on the brink of crisis, with reported levels of trust in governing institutions in long-term decline, MORI reported that only 48 per cent of people tend to trust their local council, 47 per cent the British parliament, 45 per cent the civil service, 43 per cent the government, and only 18 per cent politicians.

The comparative advantage of community organisations to generate different bases of legitimacy therefore places them ahead of what is a more general curve.

Disabled voters in Scotland agreed that they were more responsive to overtures from the Vote 2003 project because it was organised by Capability Scotland, an organisation that they knew and trusted, rather than being linked to a party or the Scottish executive. One drew an analogy with the experience of trying to claim benefits, when the member of staff you are talking to at the benefits' office is not disabled.

According to the receptionist at the Ashton Centre, 'even though I work here as well, people would see me primarily as a parent . . . You might be nervous about coming in, but if you get recommendations from other local people – rather than a note through the door – then that's different. That's how people see the centre.'

In Northern Ireland, the Catholic community has historically had a very difficult relationship with statutory bodies. Voluntary and community organisations like the Ashton Centre have, by necessity, acted as a kind of shadow welfare state because this community has generally been distrustful of public provision.

An important element of this different source of legitimacy is the opportunity for reciprocity. Community organisations build trust by offering people a more positive vision of their role in co-producing goods of value to others as well as themselves. The user in traditional public service provision is often cast as the 'customer', receiving a service having paid for it through taxation. When this happens it not only creates difficulties for people who are unable to 'pay' for their entitlement in this way (because of unemployment, say), it also fosters a very thin conception of citizenship, with a very limited account of the way citizens can support each other and be co-producers of public goods and services enjoyed by other people.

The missing link

Co-production offers a rich narrative about the myriad small-scale acts of participation that improve the way we and others around us experience the public realm, and that enable us to actively reshape it for ourselves. It is the process through which positive, integrated experiences of the public realm like Martin's, and many others we have come across over the last year, can be constructed.

It shows how participation is the missing link when it comes to strengthening all three pillars of the public realm. Through community organisations, co-production may give citizens the chance to reshape not only public services but civil and democratic structures as well. The challenge, then, is to create an atmosphere in which co-production can flourish – by nurturing what we call 'communities of participation'.

4. Building communities of participation

For most primary school teachers, getting a class to obey the rules can be a bit of a challenge. But at St Bernadette's School in the Yardley area of Birmingham, when it comes to recycling paper it's the pupils who have turned enforcer.

'They have become like the paper police,' one of their teachers explains. 'If someone puts a piece of paper in the recycling bin without writing on it on both sides, it's like someone's died!'

The organisation that has been busily enrolling these youngsters to the environmental cause is Brumcan, a not-for-profit community recycling scheme based in south Birmingham. As well as providing classrooms with bins and bags for waste paper and arranging for them to be collected regularly, Brumcan holds educational workshops with pupils to teach them about some of the wider issues that underpin their paper policing. Brumcan also hosts events at schools with parents and children to mark the launch of a new scheme in the school or the local area. The gusto with which pupils take to such projects influences the behaviour of their households, as children come to monitor their parents' habits with the same vigilant enthusiasm they display in the classroom. In a sense, Brumcan has managed to unleash and harness a civically minded variant of the 'pester power' so familiar to parents in supermarket checkout queues.

For Brumcan, local schools like St Bernadette's and the children that attend them are a crucial resource, and offer a clue to its underlying approach to growing, deepening and sustaining its work. Started in 1991, Brumcan's focus was and remains the provision of a kerbside community recycling service, with individual households placing certain kinds of household waste into boxes which are collected each week. The organisation has successfully expanded across a much wider area thanks to a careful process of building community interest, appetite and capacity.

This process begins with forging an agreement with a local housing or tenants' association. This agreement provides for all profits from the recycling to be split 50:50 between the association and Brumcan. This creates direct incentives for participation, energises potential local champions and builds momentum.

In the run-up to a community launch event, boxes are delivered by hand, bringing people out into the street to collect them and talk through how they might be used. The personal touch is much more effective than just leaving a leaflet and is repeated each week, as the boxes are emptied into a pedestrian-operated cart, pushed by a member of the local community.

Alongside the community recycling schemes and the educational work, Brumcan also operates a commercial recycling venture collecting waste from Birmingham offices and businesses. It also participates in the local New Deal scheme, providing job placements for the unemployed.

In fact, there are so many layers to Brumcan's approach that it is difficult to imagine how they all came to fit together. It certainly does not sit comfortably in traditional analyses of the role of community organisations in civic participation, what we called in the last chapter the 'new traditionalism'.

But this is precisely the point. Brumcan is the ultimate go-between, skilfully straddling the boundaries between private enterprise and public action, between public services and community benefit, between personal choices and shared achievements.

Brumcan has evolved an organisational model in which participation is central to everything it does, but where the kinds of participation that matter and how they are mobilised and channelled vary greatly. Brumcan creates public value not by offering a list of worthy activities and expecting people to sign up, nor by acquiring a particular institutional or sectoral label and assuming that that gives its activities public legitimacy.

Instead, it works to enrich what we call 'communities of participation' in the areas in which it works that are capable of sustaining diversity, both in the types and levels of participation people undertake, and in the institutional settings in which they are expressed.

And while Brumcan's model is very different to any of the other organisations in this study, there were enough similarities in the approaches that each took and the cumulative result of their efforts to suggest that some underlying principles might be at work.

Five characteristics

These communities of participation seem to share five characteristics:

- O authenticity
- O effectiveness
- O supportiveness
- O flexibility
- O personalisation.

Authenticity

The first is that the experience of participation is authentic. The form that participation takes is less important than that people see and feel a direct connection between what they do and what is subsequently achieved.

For the students who work with Envision, this is what particularly sets the organisation apart. Authentic is often taken to mean real, in counterpoint to the artificial or simulated relationships we often have with and within institutions. From this point of view, Envision compares very favourably with the citizenship education they receive in school, as the following comments attest:

It's more real.

Citizenship sucks. It's patronising. Telling a bunch of 17-year-olds once a week: 'Don't spit.' It's ridiculous. It's utterly ridiculous. I'm 17 now. I think by now I know what's good for me.

But the word authentic comes from the same root as 'author'. It is the experience of being authors of change that is particularly powerful, and which sets this experience apart from other types of participation such as voting. Believing that their vote will not change anything is one of the reasons many people cite for not voting in elections; in a recent poll, it was the most important reason.[17]

Although some students begin with low expectations of what their Envision group will achieve, they are often surprised by the positive end result. 'At first you don't think you can make a difference because you're only young, but you soon see that you can,' one told us.

It is particularly striking that these students feel so strongly that they can be authors of change in their community when they have so little faith in the capacity of formal political institutions or methods:

Politicians don't care about little issues in communities. It's up to us to tackle them.

We've become a nation of unfair people. We're just doing our bit to change that.

I don't understand anything to do with politics . . . I'd vote for the wrong party.

Effectiveness

The second is that participation is effective. This sounds trite, but just as it is impossible for the experience to be effective if it is inauthentic, so it is impossible for it to be authentic if it is ineffective. The organisations we have observed have not just set and met multiple objectives and satisfied overlapping demands from their various constituencies, they have also made a point of visibly documenting and representing success, not simply to fulfil obligations to their funders but to maintain the momentum that participation has created.

Brumcan not only works simultaneously to address a raft of different goals – improved educational outcomes for school children, their families and teachers; more sustainable and responsible use of resources; job opportunities for the unemployed; generating revenue for other community-based organisations – it also makes the achievement of those goals visible. For example, the profits channelled back into housing associations are often used to create a visible symbol of what the private activities of each household have achieved for the public realm as a whole, like paying for an improvement to the local housing estate.

Supportiveness

The third characteristic is supportiveness. Another omission in the 'new traditionalist' account is the assumption that individuals can spontaneously become more civically responsible once they are given the opportunity to do so. But as de Tocqueville's metaphor of community associations as 'great free schools' suggests, people do not necessarily enter the public realm armed with the knowledge, skills and motivation they need to thrive within it. People need to be supported in acquiring the social skills that are a precondition for full participation. In Philip Agre's restatement of the classic 'give a man a fish . . .' metaphor, 'You can give people social capital, but it is better to teach them the skill of making social capital for themselves.'[18]

Capability Scotland, one of Scotland's largest disability organisations, applied that lesson to great effect in their year-long Vote 2003 project. The aim of the project was to encourage more disabled people to participate in the electoral process, empower them with the knowledge and confidence required, raise awareness of the needs of disabled voters and improve accessibility arrangements for future elections.

Vote 2003 started from the presumption that access to the electoral process was patchy, unequal and could not be taken for granted. They developed a series of interventions that supported disabled voters in becoming more active participants. One striking innovation was the creation of an online 'virtual polling station' that explained what voters could expect at each stage of the voting process and the help that they were entitled to ask for. This gave them an opportunity to practise as many times as they needed to be sure they got it right on the day. The website was the first of its kind in the UK and proved hugely popular.

Flexibility

Flexibility is also vital, both for community organisations and those who use them. Organisations not only need to work with the grain of people's lives in how they design their service offerings and approaches to user participation, they also need to adapt to their changing needs and interests.

Marshall, 75, spent his working life as a draughtsman for Harland & Wolf in Belfast in the days when the company built ships out on the riverbank, piecing them together bit by bit. Today, 'everything is modular, and it all happens indoors'. Different parts of the ship can be built hundreds of miles apart, as the few remaining draughtsmen email diagrams back and forth at the touch of a button.

The Ashton Centre is helping Marshall to adapt to this new world, teaching him how to use email and the internet himself at a drop-in computer course. Now he can save money by emailing distant relatives, and buying flights online to see them.

The Ashton Centre is itself a model of the flexibility it helps its users to display. It quickly realised that the biggest barrier for the community in taking all kinds of opportunities was lack of childcare. Having started to provide this, it realised it was freeing up parents' time. In response it has begun, in the words of the chief executive, to provide 'a bit of everything', from computer courses to aromatherapy to employment.

As this diversity of provision has reached a critical mass, the Ashton Centre has been able to define itself as an organisation in terms of its constituents rather than its function. Its focus is on ensuring flexibility and responsiveness by involving the community members in designing services for themselves. Throughout, the message is that it is 'not community groups that will do things for you, it's you that can do it for yourself'.

Personalisation

Personalisation is a growing feature of contemporary political rhetoric.[19] However, for many people, the task of identifying, articulating and satisfying their individual needs is extremely challenging. The community organisations that we have been studying demonstrate the amount of time and trust it can require to help people ask the right questions of public services.

When Just Ask Us began attending a luncheon club in rural Chichester, they were undeterred by the fact that it took eight weeks for them to be approached for information. For them, this is a transaction cost in reaching the hard to reach.

One of the few important sources of employment in the Chichester area is lettuce growing. This involves substantial numbers of migrant workers, many from Portugal, who live and work in groups. They work very long hours and are often very isolated from other communities, and from public services. Just Ask Us has built up trust with this group by organising 'fun days' with them, and has since provided support for them as late as 11pm. Just Ask Us are now working with other Portuguese speakers to ensure that a range of public services are tailored to meet their needs.

For John Kingdon, Head of Environmental Health Services at Chichester District Council, Just Ask Us enables the kind of service that it is simply not possible to provide within the statutory sector:

> *We are driven by CPA [comprehensive performance assessment] targets, which we absolutely have to fit . . . There is no flexibility. The beauty of the NOF funding is that it allows the personal service, which statutory services used to provide. It's great for me; JAU can give that caring service that I don't have a budget for.*

Underlying principles

That the organisations we have studied create these kinds of participative experiences is partly a tribute to their hard work and excellence. But it cannot be explained simply in terms of specific institutional factors. We believe that beneath their disparate activities, a common set of principles may be discerned. They are these:

○ working through and as networks, to enhance resilience and flexibility

○ giving users a voice while improving the acoustics of the institutions in which they speak

○ understanding the power of hope and shared expectations of communities' capacity.

In the following chapters, we explore what these principles mean in practice.

5. Networks and the connected community

Just after 10am on Friday 20 July 2001, two gunmen from a loyalist paramilitary splinter group calling themselves the Red Hand Defenders walked into the yard behind the Ashton Community Centre in the New Lodge district of North Belfast. Seeing two men outside smoking a cigarette, the gunmen opened fire, before turning and shooting into one of the units that housed the Centre's playgroup facility. By that time of day children had already begun to arrive. Luckily no one was killed but nursery nurses and those in their care, crouching on their hands and knees, were covered in broken glass.

The attack shocked local people, with leaders on both sides of Northern Ireland's divided community united in condemnation. Despite this solidarity, the attack was potentially disastrous for the Centre unless it could rebuild people's confidence to spend time in its buildings, and quickly. So the Centre came up with the idea of turning one of its shop front units into a therapy centre providing counselling, support groups and aromatherapy to those recovering from the ordeal. The Centre was surprised by the popularity of the scheme, which encouraged it to expand the service to help those affected by the Troubles more generally. Recently they have moved on still further, with a programme aimed specifically at the large local population of former prisoners.

Through this approach the Centre has helped the community to overcome some of the trauma of its narrow escape, and of its difficult circumstances more generally. It has addressed a quite unanticipated problem and brought in new people who have subsequently taken up other opportunities the Centre has to offer.

Community platforms

The Ashton Centre's instinctive response to adversity suggests an almost effortless capacity to adapt to changing circumstances. But like a jazz musician, this ability to improvise is founded on years of hard work and discipline. Flexibility and spontaneity are made possible by determined investments in resilience and coherence.

To understand what makes this possible, we need to reach for a different way of thinking about the identity and structure of community organisations. One question that the community groups in our study found it hard to answer was 'what do you do?'. For an organisation like the Ashton Centre, the question is a bit meaningless. Partly that's because it does a great many things, not all of which it expected to be doing, many of which are a response to changing needs and circumstances. But partly it's because what the organisation does, and the part that it plays in people's lives, can't really be described in terms of the services it provides. Like the other organisations in this study, what they *do* is not what they are *for*.

Broadly speaking, each was concerned with developing and supporting the capabilities of the communities it worked with. But they did this not by defining a programme of discrete activities or functions, but by nurturing communities of participation that extended the organisation's reach and increased the range and scope of activities it could undertake. The organisation's focus was on creating a *platform* capable of sustaining diverse and sometimes even incoherent sets of activities. In other words, the difficulty many community organisations have in saying what they do is not a sign of weakness. More often than not it is a sign of strength.

At one level this is quite a provocative point. The conventional wisdom is that form follows function. While the organisations in our study were certainly responding to the needs of their community, the organisational model they have created is integral to their capacity to do this. People's needs within and across communities are diverse, complex and ever changing. Satisfying them requires a degree of 'adaptive capacity'[20] that most traditional public service organisations, based on historically defined functions and roles, do not possess.

For example, Kevin is an employee at Brumcan who arrived through the New Deal, via a series of unrewarding jobs. Like most people, his needs are multiple. First of all, he needs a viable source of employment. This is ensured by Brumcan's business recycling arm, which is able to turn a clear profit. Second, Kevin needs training and a source of additional qualifications. Through Brumcan, he can gain NVQs and vocational qualifications such as forklift truck driving. However, perhaps most importantly, Kevin wants to do a job which gives him a sense of pride that he is participating in something worthwhile. He finds his work collecting for Brumcan's community recycling – pushing an electric cart through a local neighbourhood each day – highly rewarding. As well as getting to know people in the neighbourhood, Kevin values the fact that by building up these relationships and the commitment to recycling that goes with them, he can boost his own wages, which are governed in part by the tonnage he is able to collect. He can access all these things as part of Brumcan's diverse network – only because Brumcan functions as a platform.

But as well as catering for the complexity of people's needs – a 'demand-side' pressure, as it were – operating as a platform also matters on the 'supply-side', given that the forms which people want their participation to take are also so diverse.

Nick at Envision says that in the short time the organisation has been running, 'we've learnt a lot about what a platform actually is'. In particular, he says, they've recognised that their capacity to predict or specify things in advance is strictly limited. For example, they have greatly widened the scope of their initial pitch to students, moving away from a narrowly defined focus on environmental projects to a much looser vision of sustainable development, because this better reflected what students were interested in. As the diversity of the projects schools are developing has increased, the capacity for any one person to retain an overview of the organisation's work has been commensurately reduced.

As a result, Envision has begun to invest a lot more time building relationships, since 'with these relationships we can turn on the head of a pin'.

Working through networks

The result of taking the platform model seriously is that it can become very difficult to know where the boundaries of organisations start and finish. Embedded in a web of relationships of varying types, it makes more sense to think of organisations in terms of the networks through which they work.

In Birmingham Jean and Joe are not members of Brumcan, but they are central to its success. They live on 'the island', a turning circle with a grass lawn in the centre, in the middle of a long residential street. In their own words, this is their community's 'hub', and Jean is at the centre, offering advice to local people on every kind of local public service and activity. This is how the couple came to be working with Brumcan. Brumcan understand that to make their community recycling scheme work, they need to connect it with the ways that communities already work. Not only has Jean become a vocal and enthusiastic user of her black box, she helps and cajoles others in her street until they too are equally enthusiastic.

At Just Ask Us, people like this are the bedrock of their organisation. In the words of Nicola Day, responsible for uploading information to help tackle rural isolation, the key point is that these people 'are doing it already'.

A new vocabulary

Working as platforms broadens organisational reach, and strengthens capacity to meet the evolving needs of its users. It also keeps organisations fleet-of-foot, preventing them from becoming too fixated on the provision of any single activity or service or too dependent on particular sources of funding.

But this notion of platforms is at odds with the dominant conception of community groups held by government and many funding bodies. In the first place, it necessarily implies a high degree of unpredictability about exactly which direction (or more likely directions) a community group's activities will go in. Contractual service provision typically involves a much clearer specification of activities in advance. The experience of the organisations in our study was that grant giving had usually afforded more flexibility: 'Yeah, you go in there and you tell them about the project and this is what we're doing and they're like, "that sounds great, go away and do it". But this is not a view universally shared across the sector, as an earlier Demos report made clear.[21]

Second, it challenges some of the usual aphorisms, often voiced in response to the apparent encroachment of an audit culture in all sectors, about the need to measure 'outcomes' rather than 'processes'. While we might empathise with this suspicion of performance measurement regimes, in this context it is not clear that a focus on outcomes really helps, because it is likely that desirable outcomes cannot be specified in advance. It was sobering to hear from Capability Scotland that with hindsight they might have scaled back their stated objective of increasing electoral participation among disabled voters, on the basis that it turned out to be too difficult to prove either way. Third, what this suggests is that we need a new vocabulary for talking about community organisations, assessing funding bids and evaluating success that is aligned with the underlying characteristics of community groups as platforms.

6. Voice, and making it count

For Alan, voting is the ultimate expression of his democratic citizenship, representing not just the right to participate in elections but the responsibility to help and encourage others to do likewise.

Yet he realises voting can be a hugely daunting and confusing experience for many people, not least with the introduction of new institutions like the Scottish Parliament and new voting methods based on proportional representation. Some voters believe they are insufficiently knowledgeable to make a well-informed decision. Ballot papers are now more complex. Polling stations, the hidden plumbing of the electoral system, are invariably located in schools, churches and other buildings designed for very different purposes.

And most of these problems are experienced even more acutely if, like Alan, you happen to be disabled.

Capability Scotland realised that campaigning for fair access to democracy was about more than changing the fabric of polling stations. To change behaviour, they had to be able to hold two conversations simultaneously – with those running the election and with disabled people themselves. Above all, they needed to build legitimacy among the disabled voters they aspired to represent.

To achieve this, they set in train three key processes. First, they established the '1 in 4' poll, a regular feedback survey involving thousands of disabled people offering their opinions, advice and constructive criticism of the organisation's work. Because the group was so large, Capability Scotland could create incentives for participation simply by enabling them to communicate with each other. Each time they fed back the results of a questionnaire or consultation, they provided the group with the stimulus to participate in the next one. When they came to develop their Vote 2003 project, Capability Scotland could not only build up a very accurate picture of democratic participation among disabled people; with their help, they were also able to craft poster and radio advertisements perfectly tailored to their audience.

But however sophisticated its advertisements, Capability Scotland knew that the most powerful advocates were disabled voters themselves – people like Alan. They saw an opportunity to arm members of the '1 in 4' poll group with the knowledge they needed to participate more actively in making change happen. By providing hundreds with a checklist for carrying out an accessibility audit of their local polling station, they enrolled them as action researchers-come-agents provocateurs. Arriving at polling stations on the day of the election, clipboard in hand, these people served to both capture valuable internal information for the organisation and to deliver the Vote 2003 message right where it was needed. As Alan puts it, 'Putting training in the packs for returning officers was a bit lackadaisical if you know what I mean. It was only when we turned up at the polling stations that they knew we meant business.'

The success of the Vote 2003 project reminds us that the ways in which community organisations help their members to be heard by society at large is often key to their success. This ability derives from a curious feature: while most organisations tend to think they have two audiences, internal and external, for community organisations the audience is part of the organisation. As a result, they can become especially adept at connecting what they do with what they think and say, an enviable quality when trust in most public institutions is in decline.

For community organisations, this is vital for two connected reasons. On the one hand, they need to be able to understand their own communities and respond to them. On the other, it also ensures that the civic participation they enable generates shared identity. Like the traditional haka of the New Zealand Maori, publicly performing a community's identity is intrinsic to sustaining it, but to do this the performance must be accurate and faithful.

Understanding the challenge

One way to illustrate this challenge is to take an example from a very different area. For the music industry, peer-to-peer file sharing is a serious problem: more and more people are simply sharing music over the internet rather than buying it in the shops. As well as reducing sales, one effect of this has been to devalue the pop charts since purchases are an increasingly inaccurate measure of people's favourite music. Without central points of distribution, the fear is we will lose a handle on what music people value, and what new talents should be nurtured.

Or rather, this was the fear. Because in the United States, a company called Big Champagne has devised a way to track, record and archive the music people share and request. As a result, for each new song, they have a real-time picture of its popularity. This means they not only have all the information traditionally available from sales, like what region fans live in, they also know what else they like to listen to. As one analyst puts it:

> Even as the industry as a whole litigates, many of the individual labels are quietly reaching out to Big Champagne, turning file sharing networks into the world's biggest focus group. In the beleaguered music business, this market research strategy that dare not speak its name is fast becoming the Nielsen ratings of the peer-to-peer world.[22]

For our purposes, what is interesting about this example is that this information does not come from prices or purchases made in markets. Instead, Big Champagne has tapped into different ways of defining and measuring value, based on what people are getting excited about. What's more, the information Big Champagne has created about their community is so powerful, even those who wish it did not exist cannot ignore it.

If the public value of civic interactions could be captured so comprehensively, it would become a force of huge democratic power, too accurate to be ignored. There again, the information cannot derive from market exchange. Nor can it come strictly from traditional representative institutions.

While we are not there yet, Vote 2003 and the other projects in our study showed how – by integrating issues of personal welfare, local concern and governance – it becomes possible not just to give people a voice, but to improve the acoustics of the institutions in which it is expressed.

Knowing your community

The trick in many of the community organisations we visited was building a reputation for knowing their community better than anyone else.

The clearest example of this is Just Ask Us. As an organisation founded to provide information about services and opportunities across rural Chichester, their knowledge of their community is their primary asset.

The problem with rural Chichester is that the costs of spreading information are so large. When they began, Just Ask Us put up their posters on village noticeboards, before realising that seemingly every other organisation was already represented there. This showed them that they had to do more. Using information support workers, Just Ask Us has gradually 'infiltrated' the various settings where people do gather, like the few community centres, luncheon clubs and farmers' markets.

In doing so, they have created a vital economy of scale. For example, the area's pensioners' support service has just two staff. They cannot possibly sustain relationships across the district over a long period, but when they need to get vital information out to elderly people, short-term efforts at creating them are simply too difficult.

By working with Just Ask Us, the number of people claiming the

Pensioner's Tax Credit in rural Chichester increased by 56 per cent between October 2003 and July 2004. As a result of these successes, demands to piggyback on the informational networks the organisation has created have followed one after the other. In the words of Nicola Day at Just Ask Us, their new 'roadshow' has led to 'numerous enquiries from organisations wanting to join the bandwagon for next year'.

However, most interesting about Just Ask Us is the fact that these external partners also comprise its governing committee. The council, primary care trust and other local bodies all helped to found the organisation. As a result, they are all well placed to receive information back from Just Ask Us. According to John Kingdon at Chichester District Council, 'Just Ask Us can pick up issues that corporately as a council we should think about . . . Their input certainly enriches the process of our corporate planning.'

In a similar way, Brumcan allows community conversations to become increasingly public. The newsletter they insert into their black recycling boxes is used increasingly by other organisations to reach their constituents. The public works that housing associations are able to fund from the recycling profits demonstrate – both to their own communities and to outsiders – the power of their collective effort and commitment.

However, for civic intermediaries, there are live and important dilemmas to negotiate, particularly in the case of Just Ask Us, who have cornered the market in information for rural Chichester. One striking example is of the distance Just Ask Us are willing to travel to mediate between residents in supported housing and the site warden. The trick, as ever, is to help people in the short term without building dependence in the long term.

Letting go of community voice

At Envision events, participants share the task of recording and documenting what is happening. Video cameras, for example, circulate from hand to hand, as the students interview each other about what has mattered most to them.

The skills and information participants garner from this are important because they help them to achieve the tasks they have set themselves. Each Envision team has webspace hosted by the organisation where they can put up information about the work they are doing, helping them to both coordinate and promote their work.

For Envision itself, hosting all these websites gives them and those interested in their work a window on what is happening across London. While this takes the public face of Envision out of the hands of those who run it, the gains in terms of the dialogue it enables outweigh the risks.

By holding that risk, Envision opens up its infrastructure and its authority to the use of the communities it supports. For Kierra Box, a graduate of Envision, this was all she needed: 'Personally, I was always interested in politics, but Envision gave me a forum where I could share it with other people.'

The more Kierra got involved with Envision, the more she noticed that their work was beginning to legitimate her and her friends as activists more generally. Others, including their teachers, began to bring issues to the group, urging them to act or asking for advice. Soon after, Kierra and her friend Rowena Davies founded Hands Up For Peace, an anti-war group for young people, which displayed handprints from thousands of young people in Parliament Square on the day that war was declared against Iraq.

The voice of the bazaar

In the cathedral, there are strict rules about who speaks and when, but the acoustics are fantastic. In the bazaar, there is a liberating free-for-all, but often, it is hard to hear yourself speak, let alone other people. Leading community organisations are increasingly showing that as community networks change and grow, while life may feel more chaotic, the potential for our democracy grows too.

7. Hoping well

Participation and the power of expectations

Jean and Joe have lived in the same house in Small Heath in Birmingham for the last 40 years. The couple are self-confessed 'hubs' of the local community. They ran a residents' association for many years, eventually succeeding in getting a problem family removed from the area. Jean is involved in a vast array of activities and committees, from the community safety partnership to Homewatch to the ward advisory board.

So when a plan emerged to revamp a barren area of the local park into a community garden with the help of celebrity gardener Charlie Dimmock and her BBC TV show *Charlie's Garden Army*, it was no surprise that Jean and Joe were quick to sign up. Given the make-up of the local community, it was decided that the garden should have a multicultural theme, blending Islamic influences in a traditional British setting to create a 'Mogul Garden'.

The plans were ambitious. The centrepiece was to be a grand, star-shaped water fountain, intricately tiled to create a sky blue mosaic. To the side of it, a brightly coloured pergola would create an archway that would eventually be covered by flowers to create a dappled light effect. This in turn would lead to an ornately decorated pavilion, designed on an Islamic theme by students from De Montfort University. Finally there would be a tall, elegant stone obelisk, a monument to those of all nationalities who had fought in the Second

World War, with an inscription in English, Bengali and Urdu 'to those who conquered in the name of peace'.

The work was supposed to take three months. In the end, bad weather meant it took closer to four. During this time, just 12 committed volunteers (Jean and Joe, of course, being among them) undertook the bulk of the work, though warm weather and the presence of TV cameras helped to bring people out at key points, and in all 300 people lent a hand at some point. Most often, these people were not close friends, but were brought together by the occasion. As the transformation of the garden began to take shape it seemed that more people were more and more prepared to believe that their efforts would be worthwhile.

Finally it was finished, and ready to be opened to the public at a special celebration, complete with musicians to provide a suitable soundtrack and chefs on hand to cook some authentic Asian cuisine. The day, filmed for the TV show in glorious summer sunshine, was a vibrant and fitting way to crown an incredible local achievement. Small Heath was not a community brimming with the social capital, social ties and networks between people, and the mutual trust that emerges from them, that social scientists like Robert Putnam consider so important for communities to work together effectively. Yet the leadership and energy of local people had made it possible.

But three days after the park opened the monument was vandalised and toppled over, and the pavilion burnt to the ground. The damage amounted to £17,000; countless more if the hours that Jean, Joe and the others had put in were included. None of the local people who helped build the park will now go near it. It is not just that it is dirty and unsafe, they say: it is because of what it represents. 'They took the heart out of it,' says Jean. The built environment, rather than being a source of inspiration, has become a monument to failure and wasted effort.

So would Jean and Joe ever do something like this in the future? They shake their heads: 'Never again'. But they look to Naz, a young Asian woman who was instrumental in getting people involved in the project, as one of a new generation that will be able to carry on their work, and who may have more stomach for the disappointments that seem almost inevitable.

Jean and Joe's story of hopes built and then dashed is one that will be regrettably familiar to anyone involved in community development. But it points to some important practical and theoretical lessons.

It's about more than social capital

The first is that the current preoccupation in policy-making circles with *stocks* of social capital is almost certainly misplaced. In Small Heath Park, despite relatively limited stocks of social capital, the community was able to cooperate to achieve something really profound. The catalyst was not the social ties among them but shared *expectations* that participation would result in meaningful change. In this case, it seems likely that these expectations were bolstered by the presence of television and celebrity, and the scrutiny and resources that they would naturally bring to bear. But it also suggests that these shared expectations or beliefs are a precious quality that has to be carefully nurtured and sustained. When they are undermined, as the example shows, it can seriously affect the likelihood of effective community action in the future.

To see why, despite the policy consensus of the day, the notion of social capital is far from the elixir of community life, it is useful to look at the origins of the metaphor of capital. In economics, a firm that tried to maximise its capital would be in very serious trouble. Here, the real imperative is profitability, which is governed by a whole range of factors – labour, exchange, the list is endless. Therefore, even in a sphere where the notion of capital is unquestioned, how and when to accumulate it remains an open question. In the case of social capital within communities this is even more certain. As well as who knows whom, how people engage with one another, the work that they do together and what they believe about it are clearly vitally important.

We need to build hope

Staying with the analogy of economics, we know that what people believe is often as important as the stocks of capital they hold, a point captured by John Maynard Keynes's wonderful description of the 'animal spirits' on which successful economies depend:

> *A large proportion of our positive activities depend on spontaneous optimism rather than mathematical expectations . . . Most, probably, of our decisions to do something positive, the full consequences of which will be drawn out over many days to come, can only be taken as the result of animal spirits – a spontaneous urge to action rather than inaction.*[23]

A climate of fear can lead to a run on the banks and a paralysis of exchange, while pessimism can see spending stagnate.

This is equally true in communities. Without the hope that animates social networks, for example, social capital can go to waste. The networks people have are only as valuable as what they believe they can accomplish through them. And unlike Keynes's animal spirits, these civic spirits are perhaps not so spontaneous, and must be carefully nurtured.

This point helps to explain why the creeping privatisation of our personal hopes – illustrated in the growing gap shown in chapter 2 between personal and collective optimism – matters so much. The combination of social networks and shared expectations for successful collective action has been called 'collective efficacy'. As American sociologist Robert Sampson puts it:

> *Use of the term collective efficacy is meant to signify an emphasis on* shared beliefs in a neighbourhood's capability for action to achieve an intended effect, coupled with an active sense of engagement on the part of residents *[our emphasis]. Some density of social networks is essential, to be sure, especially networks rooted in social trust. But the key theoretical point is*

that networks have to be activated *to be ultimately meaningful.*[24]

In other words, a realistic belief that shared action can make a difference can itself make a difference. The most successful community organisations are those that enable local social engagement *and* build the belief that communities can have an impact. It is certain kinds of network that bring the two together.

In the New Lodge, North Belfast, the importance of shared hope seems to be ingrained in the local community. The New Lodge is surrounded by 'interfaces' with protestant communities, which can be barriers to opportunity and flash points for trouble. As the manager of the nursery at the Ashton Centre, Anja, comments, 'interface violence is ongoing, and probably a long way from stopping'. However, she says, while 'people write off the area, "ah, it's only the New Lodge" . . . some of them can't write it off'. As Studs Terkel writes, 'some people have the luxury of losing hope',[25] but people in New Lodge do not.

Our survey data showed that of the five organisations we studied, those using the Ashton Centre were the most hopeful about the future. Remarkably, they were also the least trusting both of public institutions and people generally.

It is particularly difficult for the community organisation in the New Lodge to build hope because the physical space in which it can grow is so constrained. Because land is so closely contested between Catholic and Protestant communities, there is very little space in which to establish new or shared resources such as nursery places, even when the shared will and money for them has been found.

A plot of land in the New Lodge has recently been freed up for development, but first in line to build on it is a chain of amusement arcades. The community is concerned that, far from 'providing jobs', the arcade might add to the New Lodge's social and economic problems. The Ashton Centre has been instrumental in the early stages of mobilising opposition to the arcade, and making representations to the council on the community's behalf. As attempts at community development can be systematically frustrated, maintaining hope in the power of their common endeavour is vital in helping the community to sustain itself.

This has important implications for funders and for policy-makers. Rather than simply trying to increase stocks of social capital, a task which in any case government knows remarkably little about,[26] it is important to develop policy interventions that are likely to have a positive and lasting impact on both levels of engagement on the part of local people *and* their shared beliefs in the neighbourhood's capability for action. As we will see, the record in addressing these challenges simultaneously is mixed at best.

Hope has to be managed effectively

Building hope is a complex task, which happens gradually over a long period. It differs from 'aspiration-raising' in two ways. First, it is symmetrical; it means policy-makers and others, as well as community members themselves, gradually build positive expectations about their capacity to make a difference. This reciprocal quality is vital both to the development of public trust and to the ability to withstand setbacks and disappointments.

Second, it must be realistic hope. Today, people are increasingly influenced by those around them, their own friends and family. With hopefulness grounded in personal experience, it is more important than ever that community organisations model and celebrate the potential of collective action. However, people's expectations can still be wildly different or out of line with reality.

Returning to our economic analogy, we know that this can be dangerous. Gaps between different people's expectations, or expectations and reality are an important factor in economic downturns and depressions. Equally, when hopes are built up in the short term only to be dashed, like good crops ploughed under, what social capital there is can go to waste. The story of Small Heath Park is a powerful example of this.

Making these connections between people and the situations of which they are a part is therefore an important task for community organisations. They do this best by modelling the connections themselves, integrating the support they provide in helping people to cope with the work they do to engender hope. Here, all community organisations will face difficult dilemmas. There is an art to hope, not only for individuals but also for whole communities, and it is a difficult one to master.

One example of such a dilemma is provided by Envision. In contrast to those who use the Ashton Centre, the young Envision participants were among the most trusting of other people, but were the least hopeful about the future. To an extent, this is a validation of the Envision mission: to dispel not young people's supposed apathy but their pessimism and hopelessness, confident that activism will follow.

Indeed, despite their general pessimism, when asked whether, if they worked together, the communities of which they were a part could make a difference, Envisionaries were among the most positive. This is the very specific kind of hope that Envision has sought to build, scaffolding activities through which young people learn about the potential of activism and how to unlock it.

In truth, the founders of Envision believe that it does not matter if activists fail; they will learn from the process. Their instinct is to let the teams go it alone because they will learn more in the process, even if they end up biting off more than they can chew. However, they also know the power of further success to spur further activity.

For example, the Envision team at Queen's Park School have set themselves an extremely ambitious objective. Students in the group, called Juvenescence, have spotted a small church across the road from the school field, deserted and boarded up. They are seeking to turn it into a sixth form youth club, study centre and internet café. Having encountered understandable wariness from teaching staff, the students have gone over their heads, working with the Mayor of Brent and the Kensal Consultative Forum to start to win the resources and permissions that this will require. In their quest to find allies, the students have struck up dialogue with local residents, for whom the building is a problem, as a site of drug use in an otherwise desirable area. However, this project will take more than a year, the life of the current Envision team. They will have to find successors from within their school to take on the work, and sustain themselves through difficult months of obstruction and bureaucracy. The challenge for Envision is to guide them through this, working at every stage to build both realism and hope into the work they do.

Connecting the personal and collective

Just as the best schools hope to connect the ambitions of a thousand aspiring young astronauts with real opportunities, so community organisations provide local channels through which people can make their personal choices count in ways that are formative of shared civic responsibility. By acting as intermediaries for organising, mediating and pooling acts of participation, no matter how small scale, they contribute to an overall atmosphere of hope in the possibility of collective action that makes those experiences more meaningful and more likely to be repeated.

From what we have learnt from these five organisations, it is clear that this atmosphere does not develop by accident. It is deliberately fostered through the approach that they take; it could be enriched further and faster if other elements of the institutional landscape embraced its potential. How we unleash the full potential of communities of participation to enrich and sustain our public realm is the subject of the next chapter.

8. Putting citizens in the driving seat

Investing in communities of participation

Mark is not having a good day. He would like to be getting on with his job running the Ashton Centre's ICT literacy programmes, helping local people to develop marketable computer skills and gain accreditation through the European Computer Driving Licence scheme. But today is turning into one big distraction. The auditor has come in to check that what he has been doing is up to scratch. More accurately, the *auditors* have come in, because another auditor is also here to make sure the first one is doing his job properly. Just to be clear, there's a second auditor conducting an audit of the first auditor's auditing.

As the day wears on – and it is taking all day – Mark's frustration begins to show, particularly as the questions being asked of him seem to veer further and further away from the central issue of the quality of the service he is providing. First, the auditor needs to see a fire safety certificate, so Mark disappears to find it. But it turns out this isn't quite sufficient and that he actually needs to *see* the fire exits, so Mark wanders off again with the auditors in tow. Next, he wants to know whether the Centre owns the building they are in, to which Mark replies (with just a hint of exasperation in his voice) that not only do they own it, but that they built it themselves by knocking on every door in the New Lodge area of Belfast to raise the money. Inevitably, however, he really needs to see the actual deeds to the building and Mark goes to fetch them.

The sight of the three of them traipsing around after one another resembles a bizarre cross between *The Office* and *Benny Hill*, which brings new meaning to the phrase 'audit trail'. This feeling is reinforced by the sense that all the actors involved are giving performances, following a script that forces them to conceal their real interests or roles.

The point of this story is not to rehearse the familiar arguments about the impact of the demands for accountability placed on community organisations on their ability to do their real job, a topic which Demos has discussed elsewhere.[27] But it does force us to return to a question we began with in the introduction to this pamphlet and which has lain just beneath the surface throughout: just how good are we at recognising and valuing the contribution that public organisations make?

There's a great children's story by Allan Ahlberg, in which Mr Tick the Teacher runs a school that only his own kids attend. The children love it and want to keep it open, but one day the government inspector calls and if he doesn't like what he sees the school could be closed down. So Mr Tick's children secretly rush around from the classroom to the gym to the playground so that the inspector will think the school is full of pupils enjoying themselves, and give it a good report.

We suspect that this is an experience many people involved with community organisations in whatever capacity will recognise: the need to validate their performance in ways that seem inconsistent with or to miss the real value of their work. That, we have suggested, is their capacity to mobilise forms of participation by users and citizens which other types of institution cannot. In this chapter, we ask how lottery distribution bodies and other funders might support and nurture this capacity.

Creating a more fertile funding climate for community organisations

As they have shifted from passive benefactors to pro-active architects of the community organisations' operating environment, funding bodies have grown in policy importance. As we have argued, the job of policy is to steer and stimulate the development of long-term, organic processes of community development without putting too many obstacles in their path. As funding bodies become increasingly central to that task, it is appropriate to have a public conversation about the values and principles which underpin their behaviour. It is these principles, and the practices that embody them, on which our conclusions focus.

We have argued in this report against placing too much emphasis on the functional role of community organisations at the expense of their wider civic role – their ability to help create communities of participation locally and a participative democracy nationally. In our view, the best way for funders to understand, support and encourage these organisations is to explicitly recognise these strengths and seek to emulate them: to cultivate an approach to engaging with community organisations that reflects the way that they in turn engage with their users.

Mathematicians use the word 'fractal' to describe shapes that can be broken down into smaller parts that look the same as the whole. So the values that underpinned 'fractal funding' would be the same as the values that underpin the work of the best community organisations themselves, with funders striving to be:

○ authentic
○ effective
○ supportive
○ flexible
○ personalised.

Authenticity

The principle of independence from government is vital to the legitimacy of lottery funders and to their ability to support valuable work. However, too often, the notion of institutional independence is presented in terms of a thorny dilemma between state capture and glorious isolation. Neither option is attractive; the independence funders need is as much about connectedness to government and community activity as it is about freedom from some of the restrictions to which they themselves are subject. For example, earlier this year the Big Lottery Fund gave £12 million to the international reconstruction effort in the wake of the Asian tsunami – drawing both on their links to public opinion and the liberty their position affords. Whatever the rights and wrongs of particular decisions, only by striking this balance can lottery funders truly be authentic; only through challenging relationships with other national and local stakeholders can they find their own voice.

While much work has already been done to find this balance, challenges remain. Constitutionally independent, lottery funders have nevertheless been subject to reorganisation from government and perennial hounding from the press. In a society that demands instant political results, the consequences of this are clear. Research for the Big Lottery Fund, based on interviews with funders from across the country, confirms the difficulty this creates: 'for lottery funders impact is complicated by the short-termism of their funding and their priorities, and the lack of certainty about their future role. As such they are concerned with gaining maximum impact from short-term financial intervention.' It seems that while we expect lottery funders to escape the relative short-termism of the five-year electoral cycle, there may be more that can be done to support them in this endeavour.

Government, lottery funders themselves and society as a whole may all be able to do more to support the principle of lottery funders' independence, and to create the practices that can model and support it. There is an interesting analogy here with the principle of free speech – while it can cause controversy, public figures tend to support it for the wider benefits it can bring. We argue that the principle of lottery funder independence is similar – its renewal is an ongoing task for our democracy. To this end, our first recommendation is that *government and lottery funders alike do more to make the case for funders' independence, forging a simple, sustainable public agreement about their remit and mission.* In doing so, the challenge is to find a settlement that guarantees funders' independence while connecting them to underlying shifts in public priorities – to create for them the freedom to break new ground without the danger that they stray too far off course.

Yet whatever lottery funders' constitutional position, this alone cannot ensure that they develop their own authentic voice. Fortunately they have a tremendous source of knowledge, insight and inspiration at their disposal to help them do so – the projects they fund. Using their understanding of the work of which they are a part, funders can create a sense of moral purpose that is clear beyond the organisation and consistent within it. To make this possible, funders must build relationships over and above those concerned with formal accountability. As a step in the right direction, our second recommendation is therefore that *all staff should spend at least one week a year 'on site' visiting projects and organisations that have been supported.*

Effectiveness

We have argued that participation is both an end in itself and the key to many of the fundamental political challenges of our time. This suggests an approach to funding that places the building of communities of participation at its heart. However, many existing measures of participation are as much a part of the problem as the solution. Not only do numbers of participants or a project's popularity not tell the whole story, too often these figures can become ends in themselves, distorting the approaches of funders and community organisations alike. As we have argued, the value of community organisations is that they are able to start with the people that they serve. In relation to participation, no performance indicator is likely to survive transformation to a target.

This is not simply to repeat the familiar plea for 'outcomes' rather than 'output' measurement. For the difficulty of defining measurable outcomes for the impact of community work is significant, and there is the same danger of starting off trying to make the important measurable, only to end up making the measurable important.[28] We heard a sobering story from Capability Scotland about the need sometimes to plan projects back to front – to think about what you want to be able to prove you have done at the end, and design your objectives accordingly. This reflects their experience of Vote 2003, where having set themselves the goal of improving turnout among disabled voters they subsequently discovered this would be nearly impossible to prove.

Many funders and community organisations alike go through cycles of animation about making clear assessments of their effectiveness followed by disillusionment about the possibility of ever achieving this. Too often, they are trying to achieve the impossible – to reproduce the lives of service users on a spreadsheet. What funders can do, and which is also our third recommendation, is *to make the process of forming judgements about the projects they fund more open and more effective*. This might be achieved by working with other local agencies and organisations to evaluate their collective impact on a particular area, and to make a conscious effort to communicate this evidence back to local people. It might involve working with service users and local community members to create accessible directories containing samples or case studies of the kind of impact their work can have or has had in that area. Over time, they might look to develop local 'near-peer' advisory groups that would capture and harness local views of the work their projects do.

Flexibility

However, funders must not simply evaluate, they must learn – and contribute to the learning of others. In addition to development and research capacity, this learning will be impossible without diversity and innovation. One way that funders can judge themselves therefore is in terms of their success in creating space in which community organisations and others can experiment and learn. For example, Vanessa Potter of the Big Lottery Fund has suggested that they would be failing were 10–20 per cent of the projects they funded not to fail.[29] Experimentation must be cautious – taking the utmost care with the lives of service users – but *a duty to experiment and learn*, our fourth recommendation, *should come with the special position funders hold.* It is a further area in which funders can differentiate themselves from government provision, since almost by definition it is much more difficult to take risks with people's core public entitlements than it is with projects that are explicitly supposed to be supplementary.

Government will have to be clear and positive about the national importance of this research and development brief, just as funders will have to demonstrate its value by actively helping statutory agencies to learn from their work and to change. To some extent, the only limit on this experimentation is the imagination and creativity of funders, but a few possibilities might include:

O   The solidarity with communities thousands of miles across the globe that has been demonstrated in the British public's response to the Asian tsunami tragedy raises the possibility of a funding stream that sought to amplify local communities' sense of their capacity to act together, not just in their own interests but in the interests of others. A funder might promise to match-fund money raised by community organisations to support charitable causes abroad.

O   The Big Lottery Fund could support clusters of schools, community organisations and a major exam board to design a curriculum for citizenship education based on the principles of action learning, with students designing practical projects and drawing out the lessons from the experience.

O   The role of lottery funding as a kind of laboratory for public service innovation could be explicitly recognised by channelling funding to groups of professionals wanting to design creative experiments in service delivery.

O   While the Big Lottery Fund might not need to have a presence in graduate recruitment, it could seek to support community organisations in creating graduate or other professional development pathways focused specifically on the community sector, as in the Ethnic Minority Foundation's customised capacity-building MBA programme.

Supportiveness

There is an increasingly well-established picture of the relationship between funders and community organisations in which the former set the agenda and the latter do the work. However, this model of the relationship can limit the capacity of community organisations to deliver and of funders to learn.

There are two areas in particular where funders could disrupt this hierarchical image by providing invaluable additional support to those that they fund. First, over the last five years, an important conversation has been taking place between the voluntary and community sectors and lottery funders about the status of overhead and administrative costs. Already a great deal has been done in this area, culminating in the recent announcement that they will agree to 'legitimate overhead costs'. However, as technology increasingly changes the way community organisations work, it opens up the possibility that this conversation be taken beyond the question of who pays for community organisations' administration to the broader question of how it is done.

As the feasibility and reach of online support grows, for example, funders may increasingly be able to function as *brokers*, helping groups of community organisations to outsource technical support in ways that free up energy and resources. Equally, funders may be able to function as *networkers*, helping community organisations to work together, pooling their capacities from web design to accounting to legal advice. Indeed, for some of the smallest community organisations, this could help to ensure their viability. Finally, by moving into this area, funders may begin to open up a further role for themselves. In both Chichester and Belfast we were told, 'here, the term "voluntary *sector*" is a misnomer'. By helping community organisations to work together technically, they may be able to *support* them in thinking and learning together, building their capacity to share knowledge both with one another and with their funders. Our fifth recommendation is that *funders build on their role as facilitators, and seek new ways to help community organisations to work and to work together.* Another visible demonstration of their commitment to moving from being a funder to a supportive partner would be to provide some of these functions themselves. For example, one powerful symbolic gesture would be for the Big Lottery Fund's new offices to include some space for community organisations to use as a meeting or event space.

Second, the best way for funders to learn about their work may be to support the learning of others. Instead of simply demanding that those they fund carefully evaluate the work that they do, can they serve as a repository for advice and research tools that would enable them to do this effectively? This would both improve the quality of funders' data and help community organisations to develop their work.

One promising application of this approach is suggested by the Big Champagne example in chapter 6. We argued that Big Champagne had shown that data normally hidden from the gaze of formal statistics (in that instance, about music downloads from the internet) can come to exercise a powerful influence over the choices and decisions of the actors in a system because it taps into an underlying pattern more significant than that provided by other measures.

As this pamphlet suggests, work on the importance of collective efficacy suggests that the same is true for communities, and the levels of hope they are able to sustain.

Beneath the poverty statistics, it is clear, as Tony Vinson has argued, that 'some communities burdened by disadvantage appear more resilient than others in overcoming adversities' because of the impact of mediating forces, like community organisations, which provide people with the networks and the hope they need to tackle their own problems more effectively.[30]

For lottery funders, of course, hope has always been a key idea. We suggest that just as the hope of individual players creates funds for the National Lottery, so lottery funders play a role in fostering collective hope, by supporting the community organisations that help to build it. We suggest that making this virtuous circle visible could help to ensure the ongoing legitimacy of funders such as the Big Lottery Fund. Our sixth recommendation, therefore, is that the *funders should work with communities, local government, other funding agencies, the Office for National Statistics and the Audit Commission to create a national Social Hope Index.* Based on measures of collective efficacy designed in partnership with local people, it would offer a rich picture of the contribution that community organisations and other players make in helping neighbourhoods, even those burdened with disadvantage, retain their resilience and their belief in their shared capacity to tackle local problems.

Personalisation

The challenge of personalisation for funders is to create funding mechanisms that are not built around a very small minority of incompetent or fraudulent organisations, but to treat each as an individual. For those that may be funding thousands of organisations at any one time, this is an extremely difficult proposition. But it is also an excellent standard against which any funder can measure themselves. In doing so, funders are asking whether they can build trusting relationships. What is clear is that funders able to experiment and learn, confident in their judgement and their position, and supportive of those they fund will be better at building these trusting relationships. And as they build them, as with individuals, so their ability to make good judgements and to trust well will grow too.

There may be new approaches that funders can develop to accelerate this process. In his famous six rules for writers, George Orwell concludes by imploring his readers to 'break any of these rules sooner than say anything outright barbarous'.[31] The idea here is to harness the adaptiveness of the author, rather than treat language as intransigent. In recent years, lottery funders have been learning a similar lesson. Today, a great deal is done to ensure that funding arrangements are enabling rather than restrictive, and that in practice many funding relationships are flexible enough to cope with the uncertainty inherent in delivering projects on the ground.

That said, there is a powerful argument for making this good practice more explicit in the framing of funding principles as a symbol of this trusting approach. And given the influence organisations such as the Big Lottery Fund have on the wider funding universe, the challenge now is to build on and popularise this trusting approach. Community organisations themselves are often fearful of re-opening negotiations, fearful that money may be withdrawn, and this too must change. Our seventh recommendation is that *all funders should explore the possibility of a 'trust first' approach, writing it into the agreements they make with community organisations.* Here, the emergence of outcomes funding is an important development, but in some cases, the outcomes themselves may need to change. The very public message to community organisations should be 'if circumstances change, adapt; if your members badly need a different service, provide it'. As a safeguard, funders could ask organisations to account for any rule-breaking retrospectively, having agreed beforehand that failing to give a proper 'account' would result in a repayment of a proportion of the funding.

Conclusion

Taken together, we believe these seven recommendations would strengthen the capacity of lottery distribution bodies and other funders to support community organisations in engaging and involving users and citizens. By modelling the principles and practices which underpin the approach of those community organisations in their own work, they will help to nurture the open and inclusive communities of participation we have sought to describe.

> ### *Recommendations for funders of community organisations*
>
> 1. Government and funders themselves must make a strong public case for funders' independent status. The two need to work together to forge a simple, sustainable public agreement about the position of lottery funders, creating the

freedom to break new ground without the danger of them drifting off course.

2. All staff of lottery funders should spend at least one week a year 'on site' visiting and working in projects and organisations that their fund has supported.

3. Lottery funders should seek to make the process of reaching judgements about applicant organisations more open and effective, exploring the roles that can be played by the public and by other trusted local organisations.

4. Lottery funders should be given a duty to experiment, as a corollary of the special position that they hold. For example, lottery funders might seek to match local fundraising efforts to reward popular participation, to create an open source citizenship curriculum to develop and draw together knowledge about participation or to harness the intelligence of local professionals in fast-tracking funding to areas of greatest opportunity.

5. Funders should do more to develop their role as pro-active supporters of community organisations. They might seek to do this by brokering procurement relationships or networking community organisations together to share administrative capacity. One powerful example might be to create space for community organisations themselves in the Big Lottery Fund's new location. In this supportive role, lottery funders may increasingly be able to give voice to community organisations, helping them to share their knowledge more widely.

6. Lottery funders should make public not only their dependence on the hopes of individual players but their activism in fostering collective hope through their support for community organisations. One way to do this would be to work with communities, local government, other funding agencies, the Office for National Statistics and the Audit Commission to create a national Social Hope Index.

7. Funders should explore the possibility of developing a 'trust first' approach, enabling the organisations that they fund to change the uses they make of funding in the event of a serious and unforeseen change in local needs and circumstances. Lottery funders should play a leadership role in establishing this approach as good practice.

But there is no reason in principle why this lesson drawing should be limited to funding bodies. The implications for other institutions, including government itself, are the subject of our final chapter.

9. Participation and the integrated public realm

Bill is retired and lives with his wife in rural Chichester. But a serious heart condition which could deteriorate at any moment has made it difficult for Bill to relax and enjoy his retirement. For Bill and his wife, knowing that they could phone for help should anything happen would have provided a modicum of reassurance.

But Bill was also convinced that his landline had developed an intermittent fault, and mobile phone reception in rural Chichester is very poor. Sorting out a reliable phone line understandably came to feel like a life or death issue for Bill, yet the phone company refused to believe his claim. Like many of us, he found it hard to navigate his way around the maze of automated telephone menus, constantly being placed on hold or offered an endless series of irrelevant alternatives. He felt alienated that he couldn't talk to a real person, because his problem went so far beyond the options that he was being presented with.

When Just Ask Us started attending Bill's community group, it was a good five or six weeks before he trusted them sufficiently to ask for their help with his phone. At first his request seemed trivial. Just Ask Us agreed to look into it, and quickly resolved the problem.

The following week, Just Ask Us staff saw Bill again to check that all was well. He was grateful and glad to have his phone fixed. But he was also more willing to open up, revealing a whole range of other, much more serious health and social concerns that had been blighting his life. Just Ask Us are now helping him with mobility issues and working with him to obtain a stair-lift. In doing so, they are linking him up with services and resources that he would not previously have known how to access, and who in turn would not have known how to reach him. So preoccupied had Bill become with his phone problem that he had been unable to articulate a range of services that would prove essential to his quality of life.

For Bill, Just Ask Us staff were the first people who had ever listened to him properly. They succeeded by recognising that the best way to improve Bill's health was for Bill himself to become a more active participant in determining, clarifying and addressing his own needs.

The integrated public realm

There are times when all of us have felt a bit like Bill: faced with a compelling issue we need to resolve but unsure of how; certain that the knowledge we have must be part of the solution but struggling to find anyone who will take us seriously; casting around for some help but confronted instead with cold, impersonal institutions that don't seem interested in offering any.

In this pamphlet, we have shown that at their best community organisations can help to overcome this problem, by being more successful at mobilising the participation of their users and local citizens in the meaningful pursuit of designing and creating solutions to their needs. We have also suggested that their capacity to do this is based on certain concrete principles and practices which we have sought to make clear. In chapter 8 we examined some of the steps that lottery and other funders might take in order to support community organisations more effectively in this work.

From these conclusions, there is an opportunity to raise a wider set of questions about the environment within which community organisations operate. In this final chapter, we return to the broader canvas of the public realm which we explored in chapter 3 – governance and democratic representation, voluntary action and civil society, as well as public services. The renewal of this public realm, we have argued, sits at the forefront of contemporary political debate. And crucially, politicians on all sides are recognising for the first time that this renewal depends not on smarter or more expensive interventions from the centre but on engaging citizens as the active co-producers both of new and better services, and of the values of trust, legitimacy and transparency which they expect from them.

Students, patients and local communities, not teachers, doctors or police officers, are the 'biggest untapped reserve' in the quest to transform public services as David Miliband MP, the Minister for Communities and Local Government, has acknowledged. 'Public services can only be made safe for a generation if we engage citizens in their design and delivery,' he told a conference of public service professionals in February 2005. 'We need to put the public back into public services.'[32]

The best community organisations therefore have a capacity to mobilise participation which the rest of society increasingly thinks it needs. If that is indeed the case, then it is not enough simply to celebrate the work of community organisations, or to ask how we can help them to do their work better. We need to ask what lessons these other institutions that contribute to the public realm might learn from them: how might the principles and practices of the community organisations we have documented in this pamphlet be applied more widely, and with what implications?

Moreover if, as in Bill's case, the effect of greater citizen participation is to make a whole range of actors work harder and smarter to improve social outcomes – the voluntary and community sector, private companies, local public service providers, and, of course, citizens themselves – we need to ask how we can better understand, make sense of and structure the interactions and relationships between different institutions in order to sustain a more participatory and vibrant public realm.

Those are the questions this chapter sets out to answer, and in seeking to answer them they lead us to engage in a deliberately provocative, but we hope constructive, thought experiment about what might happen if community organisations like the ones we have studied were in a position to influence the wider systems of public service provision and democratic representation of which they are part. Rather than jumping through the funding and accountability hoops placed in their way by public agencies, what if both the way we deliver public services and the way we reach shared decisions about how to address local needs were reshaped around their special ability to engage and involve citizens?

Some of our recommendations are radical measures and longer-term priorities. But we believe that they are consistent both with the underlying principles we have explored, and with the direction of many of the broader *currents* of the political mainstream, even if some of the specific issues we address do not figure at present.

The first section looks at how government and other agencies might enhance the role of community organisations and other actors as **civic intermediaries**, helping citizens to navigate the public realm more easily and effectively. The second section looks at how we might link participation through community organisations to new rights and roles in **local democratic representation and governance**.

Civic intermediaries

In chapter 3, we surveyed the three pillars of the public realm: governance and democratic representation, voluntary action and civil society, and public services. We drew together the processes that we had seen, rebuilding and strengthening them through the notion of co-production, which recognises the vital role that citizens play in the production and ongoing reproduction of each of these pillars. In the area of public services, we saw that citizens are necessarily a factor in the quality of the services that they receive, but that this factor can be explicitly acknowledged, developed and leveraged. Not only does this lead to a better quality of service, it means that the new directions and relationships their users create can gradually transform public provision. The same, we argue, is true of our democracy and civil society – each can be reshaped by citizens so that the ways they use it or are invited to use it are more closely aligned with their lives and priorities. We also saw that community organisations currently play a vital role in enabling co-production to happen, because they are able to avoid some of the traps that other institutions fall into.

Our first four recommendations for the public realm explore how we can create a more fertile environment in which co-production can flourish.

Language and mental models of public policy

First, the language and mental models of public policy and management need to stop viewing public services as the end of a process, as words like 'delivery', 'customer' and 'end user' would imply. Instead, they should recognise that for many people public service institutions are their entry point to the public realm, not the end of it. The conversations about babysitting that happen between parents at the school gates, or the mutual support that emerges from friendships built up in the Sure Start centre, or the valuable extra services the family hears about from the health visitor – public services can be a space in which people learn both how to get more out of the public realm, and how to put more back. But that can happen only if we *enhance the role of public institutions as civic intermediaries, whose role it is to understand the needs and aspirations of citizens, help them to navigate services and institutions in order to meet them, and to reshape the character of the public realm in accordance with the kinds of encounters they have with it.*

In earlier chapters we saw what being a civic intermediary meant for the Ashton Centre, with its experimentation with a diverse range of services, its openness and responsiveness to local demands, and the high-trust relationships it enjoys with its users. For public services, there are no simple blueprints but Charles Leadbeater offers some sensible rules of thumb:

> *Moves towards user involvement and co-production are more effective when they follow a few simple rules:*
> O   *Set incremental goals, starting small and manageably.*
> O   *Specify clearly what the user and the service professionals expect to do.*

O *Keep joint records of achievement and performance to reinforce success.*

O *Give users a mix of options through which they can achieve their goals.*

O *Frame the policy in an aspirational way to excite ambition.*

O *Provide role models and peer-to-peer support to build confidence.*[33]

A new focus for audit and inspection regimes

Our second recommendation is that it would be easier for public managers to cement commitment to co-production were *audit and inspection regimes to pay explicit attention to the way that public agencies engage with the time, resources and enthusiasm at the disposal of their citizens or members.* This is not a novel view, nor one that is simple to act on. It encapsulates and extends the familiar (and increasingly popular) plea for a greater focus on high-level social outcomes over the easy to measure processes and outputs that are supposed to stand as proxies for them. It builds on the preventative tradition in health and other public services, and on earlier Demos work calling for a more 'holistic' approach to government intervention.[34]

The move to 'value-added' scores in school performance management is a welcome step in the right direction. However, these scores seek to acknowledge the public's contribution to a school's work by factoring it out rather than in (in this case, the individual student's existing resources of academic potential and family support). As an unintended result, there is a growing incentive for headteachers to talk down the communities they serve rather than talking them up. As an open challenge to Ofsted and other inspectors or regulators of public services, could a way be found so that the next generation of value-added scores treat co-production as a positive, and measure institutions' success in encouraging it?

The sharing and expression of collective choices

We saw earlier how by helping estates and neighbourhoods share in the profits of their own recycling, Brumcan worked to demonstrate the power of collective choices. This example points to another clue to the puzzle this pamphlet has explored about why the Lottery-funded organisations we studied were so successful in fostering co-production. Their ability as non-statutory bodies to start with the person rather than with their 'problems' or the existing solutions or structures seemed extremely important. They sought not just to build their members' social capital, but to understand how they themselves wanted to *use* it.

So our third recommendation is that, while working to promote greater choice for individuals, *public bodies should help communities to make visible the collective possibilities they share and to express their collective choices in ways that are meaningful to them.* They should not try to shoehorn them into structures of participation that may not be appealing to them.

This is a crucial shift in emphasis and one that should echo across Whitehall, especially when so much time and energy is being devoted to creating governance structures for giving local people more say over how things are run, despite limited evidence that they wish to use their scarce social capital in this way. For example, the overall public response suggests little enthusiasm for participating in new arrangements for governing foundation hospitals, with few people registering as 'members' and even fewer bothering to vote in board elections.[35] Public bodies should focus on enabling individuals and communities not simply to build social capital but to use it in the ways that they determine. One example of what this might mean is the introduction of 'voice vouchers' to give parents a simple, collective say in how school budget priorities are set, a proposal Demos has set out in more detail elsewhere.[36]

Improved access to information and services

Fourth, one of the biggest obstacles to public institutions acting as civic intermediaries, and helping people to build and use their social capital in more flexible ways, is the difficulty people – like Bill – have with knowing how to access them in the first place, and the difficulty the institutions have in making their services, processes and systems navigable to them once they do.

Today, technology exists to overcome this barrier to more active citizenship: what in the United States is known as a '311' telephone service, most famously adopted by the authorities in New York. The idea is pretty simple. A citizen with a question or a complaint can pick up the phone and speak to a live operator 24 hours a day, seven days a week to get the answer. The service partly supplements the emergency number 911, giving people an outlet at those tricky times when they need to speak to someone but realise it is not an emergency. More importantly it acts, in the words of author Stephen Johnson, as an 'information concierge'. There is no need to work out which of the dozens or potentially even hundreds of different bodies, agencies, departments or helplines you need to speak to. With sophisticated data-handling systems making all public information available to helpline staff in one place, they can dependably answer citizens' queries, at any time of day, in any of 170 languages. They receive tens of thousands of calls each day.

The most impressive part of the system is that the authorities are able to track information about the calls in order to learn more about their citizens' problems. Not only do they have an accurate barometer on the problems citizens are experiencing week to week, they can map the data by street, revealing weak spots in the city's public service provision or infrastructure before any one person ever sees them. According to Johnson, 'Already, 311 data is changing the government's priorities. In the first year of operation, noise was the number one complaint [in New York], the Bloomberg administration subsequently launched a major quality-of-life initiative combating city noise.'[37]

But perhaps the most exciting thing about 311 is not that it would necessarily put an end to frustrating experiences like Bill's. It is the potential value it would be to a community organisation like Just Ask Us in connecting with citizens more quickly, easily and effectively. As we learnt earlier, they found it very difficult initially to spread the word about their services because they were jostling with so many others for attention. With a system like 311, Just Ask Us, alongside a raft of other information about community issues, events, opportunities and resources that citizens might be interested in, could be just a phone call away.

In the same way that the first street maps enabled people to explore the public spaces of their cities properly for the first time, so a 311 service could make a crucial contribution to helping citizens enjoy and participate in the public realm. Our fourth recommendation *is that local councils should invest in open source 311 systems*, constructed and continuously updated with the help not just of local public agencies but the community and voluntary sector too, thus increasing their expectations of what the public realm can offer and allowing them to engage with their community organisations anytime, anywhere.

Democratic representation and local governance

We have seen that community organisations are able to mobilise people in many different ways, as service users or carers, neighbours or volunteers, consumers or voters. Yet despite the fact that these experiences are arguably richer than traditional forms of political participation, they often do not count when it comes to formal democratic representation. That is because the links between the forms of engagement community organisations permit and the traditional rights, roles and responsibilities of formal governance institutions are often fragile at best. Dropping a slip of paper into a ballot box from time to time is increasingly unsatisfactory as the sole expression of our citizenship, yet for now we have no effective way of translating other forms of participation into representative democratic practice.

If part of the challenge is to encourage communities not simply to build social capital but to use it, then helping people to understand more clearly *how* getting involved gives them more say over collective decisions that affect their lives matters a great deal. Our public and democratic infrastructure needs to model the links not just between involvement and sociability, but also between involvement and empowerment.

To that end, we propose four recommendations to link the capabilities vested in community organisations to new roles and rights of democratic representation.

Right of initiative

Recent experiments in electoral reform have focused primarily on the act of voting itself, such as all-postal ballots, e-voting and extended hours of polling. But the evidence suggests that these technical fixes are only part of the answer. Whether and how citizens are mobilised to participate is equally crucial.[38] We have seen that community organisations are able to engender forms of participation and trust that arguably elude other institutions, such as political parties and public bodies. To ensure that this capability accrues the greatest possible democratic dividend, our fifth recommendation is that, subject to certain checks and safeguards, *if local communities can demonstrate sufficient popular support they should be granted a right of initiative to propose a local intervention and require local authorities to bring forth a proposal and vote on it.*

The right of initiative is already recognised as a powerful form of citizen empowerment in a mass democracy, creating a more direct linkage between voters and representative institutions. Its inclusion in the draft European Constitution reflects its potential value in providing alternative channels of participation beyond conventional forms of representation.

In most cases, however, a right of initiative is triggered by the collection of individual signatures (either an absolute threshold or a certain proportion of the electorate). The lasting impact on communities and the formation of social capital is arguably therefore rather limited. You could draw an analogy between the commitment of someone signing a petition when stopped in the street compared with someone participating in a strike, march or protest.

To create a stronger relationship between more responsive governance systems and community participation, we propose that the right of initiative should be subject to a dual condition: it would need to be signed by a certain number or proportion of the local electorate, and countersigned by a certain number of community organisations. In this way, the initiative would directly incentivise the interactions between individuals and community-based organisations which, we've argued, help to build connections between people *and* shared hope in their capacity to use them to achieve common goals. Instead of asking people simply to support a proposition, it would invite them to join and identify with a community of interest which could form the basis for lasting bonds and commitment.

The effect of this proposal would be to strengthen both the deliberative and representative aspects of participation. It would enable community organisations to become issue 'hubs', drawing people into circles of debate and deliberation. It would give those organisations and the people they represent more clout and leverage in their interactions with governance institutions. And it would make it more likely that, regardless of the outcome, local people would identify more readily with decisions and the process through which they have been made. As a first step, this approach might be piloted in a specific policy area such as planning.

Participatory budgeting

Our sixth recommendation is that *government, local authorities and community organisations should initiate a series of experiments with participatory budgeting.* The high levels of participation among council house tenants in votes over whether to transfer housing stock to housing association ownership demonstrates the intuitively appealing point that people are more likely to get involved when they recognise that the issue is one that matters to them directly, and when they believe their involvement has the potential to influence the outcome.[39] We also know that on an individual level, ownership of assets transforms people's capacity for hope, making it easier for them to think positively and constructively about their future. This explains why, for example, it appears to have such an impact on their propensity to save and invest, and why 'asset-based welfare' has become an increasingly important plank of government plans for promoting social mobility.[40]

We propose to apply these two lessons to one of the most crucial aspects of local governance – budgeting and priority-setting. Although the principle of community involvement and consultation is now embedded in most regeneration and neighbourhood renewal policies, communities often report feeling disempowered by these processes and deprived of any real opportunity to influence the outcome. The temptation is to rely on the energy of a few already-overburdened community representatives as evidence of community involvement, without yielding any sense of wider ownership over the outcome.

Craig has recently argued that alongside the emphasis on individual 'choice' for parents and students we should also model collective 'voice' through a vouchers scheme that would give school users a say over how a slice of the school's budget was used.[41] This kind of participatory budgeting is most developed in Brazil, where cities like Porto Alegre have energised whole neighbourhoods to get involved in making decisions about local priorities. Although there has been some interest shown by local authorities in the UK in these approaches,[42] not nearly enough is being done to trial them in practice. One route for encouraging this might be through establishing a dedicated Beacon Council Award for participatory budgeting.

Joint bidding for government funds

Our seventh recommendation is that *local political parties, working in partnership with community organisations, should be able to bid for government funds, managed jointly by the Department for Constitutional Affairs and the Home Office, to support innovative political literacy and citizen engagement projects.* When people are distrustful of politicians, there is a temptation to engineer the politics out of public life and to seek refuge in claims to independence and impartiality. But as the furore that greeted the Hutton Report demonstrated, there is sometimes simply no escaping the need for a proper political debate. In their work with disabled voters, Capability Scotland was absolutely clear on that point.

From that point of view, low levels of political literacy – fewer than half of the electorate claim to know their MP's name, claim to know about politics or the role of MPs or would be able to pass a test of certain key political facts[43] – and the parlous state of many local political parties[44] is deeply worrying. Some people propose state funding of national political parties as the solution to this problem, but once again this falls into the trap of taking an organisational context and purpose as given, rather than thinking creatively about what people might actually want from this particular institution. We suggest, instead, that local parties be encouraged to engage with community organisations to develop grass-roots initiatives for engaging local electors and improving their knowledge and understanding of political issues and processes.

Funds for lawful protest

Our eighth and final recommendation is arguably the most provocative. It is prompted, in part, by the images of orange-clad protestors occupying Maidan Nezalezhnosti, the central square in Kiev, as the Ukrainian election controversy unfolded in the final weeks of 2004. Those scenes remind us that, though we should look to strengthen the links between community participation and formal governance, we should also remember that one of the historic functions of a vibrant civil society has been to act as a check on the exercise of illegitimate or overweening power by the state. So while it is important for community organisations to be more effective partners, sometimes strengthening the public realm may require them to be more effective adversaries. We saw earlier in this report about how seriously the Ashton Centre took on a protest role, campaigning against an unpopular local planning decision and organising its own inquiry into the killings of a number of local men in the 1970s.

Protest, as well as participation, is a sign of a healthy democracy, and sometimes the fastest route to change. As one respondent to a Big Lottery Fund consultation put it:

The Brixton riots were one of the best recent examples of a mechanism for social change that we know of. In fact, riots are excellent mechanisms for social change in the right cultural context. However, funders cannot fund riots.[45]

But if we really wanted to test the resilience of our public realm, we could find ways to support legitimate protest. Of course, there would be no simple way to set criteria to determine which causes were supported and which were not without instantly attracting an accusation of bias that would undermine the whole scheme.

There is, however, one mechanism at our disposal that would get round that: a lottery. *Organisations seeking to mount a lawful protest could enter a government lottery to receive small grants to support their cause.* Pro-hunt campaigners would have the same chance as anti-war marchers, a local residents group against the siting of a mobile phone mast the same chance as an environmentalist group against a road-building decision.

By definition, this would result in some causes receiving funding that many or even most people disagreed with – indeed, in part this is the object of the exercise. For at a time when government stands accused of authoritarianism, what better way to demonstrate a commitment to liberal democracy than to offer direct support to those who seek to criticise it?

Conclusion

These recommendations reflect the challenge with which this pamphlet began: to imagine a public realm whose institutions all understood the process of citizen participation as deeply as the community organisations we have studied over the last year seem to do, and to work through the sometimes radical implications for those institutions today.

Political leadership, and the willingness of politicians to think differently about the unique contribution community organisations make, will play a large part in determining whether this public realm comes to be realised. As we argued in chapter 3, civic participation is more and more crucial in fulfilling aspirations for renewing the public realm, but harder and harder to engineer.

The most successful community organisations do offer a way to help them past this dilemma, but only if they stop treating them as simply a means to an end and respect them as partners with invaluable knowledge and experience to bring to the shared project of creating a more vibrant, participative public realm.

In part that is because the legitimacy of political power itself is questioned as never before, and needs to be renewed through new and strengthened forms of democratic participation. For the time being, it is clear that too many people view politics the same way as the Envisionaries back at Finsbury Park do. When we ask the students whether they think of themselves as political, they shake their heads furiously and one girl, who has barely spoken to us all day, says softly: 'We want to help the people who aren't in power, not the people who are.' Let's hope future political leaders can change her mind.

Notes

1   T Blair, speech to the annual conference of the Women's Institute, London, 7 June 2000.
2   M Woolcock, 'The place of social capital in understanding economic and social outcomes' (2000); available at: www.isuma.net/v02n01/woolcock/woolcock_e.pdf (accessed 17 May 2005).
3   See, for example, T Skocpol, *Diminished Democracy?* (Norman, OK: University of Oklahoma Press, 2003).
4   Saguaro Seminar on Civic Engagement in America (2000), *Better Together: The report of the Saguaro seminar* (2000); available at: www.bettertogether.org/ (accessed 17 May 2005).
5   A Milburn, 'The politics of localism', speech to Demos, 21 Jan 2004.
6   D Marquand, *The Decline of the Public* (Tunbridge Wells, Kent: The Polity Press, 2004).
7   P Hall, 'Social capital: a fragile asset' in Perri 6 (ed), *The Wealth and Poverty of Networks*; Demos Collection 12 (London: Demos, 1997); P Hall, 'Social Capital in Britain', in *British Journal of Political Science* 29 part 3 (July 1999).
8   Home Office Communication Directorate, *Active Citizens, Strong Communities – Progressing civil renewal* (2003); available at: www.homeoffice.gov.uk/docs2/activecitizens.pdf (accessed 17 May 2005).
9   Active Citizenship Centre, see: www.active-citizen.org.uk (accessed 17 May 2005)
10 This is described in chapter 9.
11 T Bentley and J Wilsdon, *The Adaptive State* (London: Demos, 2003).
12 D Wanless, *Securing Our Future Health: Taking a long-term view* (London: HM Treasury, 2002).
13 Quoted in 'Social Exclusion Unit: Reducing re-offending by ex-prisoners' (Office of the Deputy Prime Minister); see: www.socialexclusionunit.gov.uk (accessed 17 May 2005).
14 The Carnegie Trust supports grassroots social action initiatives, including a

range that supports young people in forging their own solutions to shared challenges; see: www.carnegietrust.org.uk/ (accessed 19 May 2005).

15   MH Moore, *Creating Public Value: Strategic management in government* (Bridgewater, NJ: Replica Books, 1997).

16   D Jay, *The Socialist Case* (London: Faber and Faber, 1938).

17   Flash EB 161, European Elections 2004 Barometer; available at: www.europarl.eu.int/press/Eurobarometer/pdf/en/unitedkingdom.pdf (accessed 17 May 2005).

18   PE Agre, 'The Practical Republic: Social skills and the progress of citizenship', in A Feenberg and D Barney (eds), *Community in the Digital Age* (Lanham, MD: Rowman and Littlefield, 2004).

19   C Leadbeater, *Personalisation through Participation* (London: Demos, 2004).

20   Bentley and Wilsdon, *The Adaptive State*.

21   T Bentley, H McCarthy and M Mean, *Inside Out: Rethinking inclusive communities* (London: Demos, 2003).

22   According to Jeff Howe, writing in *Wired Magazine*, October 2003, see: www.wired.com/wired/archive/11.10/fileshare.html (accessed 17 May 2005).

23   JM Keynes, *The General Theory of Employment, Interest and Money* (London: Macmillan, 1931).

24   R Sampson, 'Neighbourhood and community: collective efficacy and community safety', in *New Economy* (July 2004).

25   S Terkel, *Hope Dies Last* (New York: The New Press, 2003).

26   Perri 6, 'Your friendship networks', in H McCarthy, P Miller and P Skidmore (eds), *Network Logic* (London: Demos, 2004).

27   See Bentley et al, *Inside Out* and P Brickell, *People Before Structures* (London: Demos, 2000).

28   D Wiliam, 'An overview of the relationship between assessment and the curriculum', in D Scott (ed), *Curriculum and Assessment* (Greenwich, CT: JAI Press, 2001).

29   *Regeneration and Renewal* (February/March 2004).

30   T Vinson, *Community Adversity and Resilience: The distribution of social disadvantage in Victoria and New South Wales and the mediating role of social cohesion* (Richmond, Vic, Australia: Jesuit Social Services, 2004); see also. http://acl.arts.usyd.edu.au/jss/ (accessed 18 May 2005).

31   G Orwell, 'Politics in the English language', in *Shooting an Elephant and Other Essays* (Harmondsworth: Penguin, 1946).

32   D Miliband, 'Putting the public back into public services', speech to Guardian Public Services Summit, Sopwell House, St Albans, Herts (Feb 2005).

33   Leadbeater, *Personalisation through Participation*.

34   Perri 6, *Holistic Government* (London: Demos, 1997).

35   P Skidmore and K Bound, 'Mapping governance at the local level', unpublished paper for Joseph Rowntree Foundation Governance and Public Services Committee (2004).

36   J Craig. *Schools Out: Can teachers, social workers and health staff learn to live together* (London: Hay Group, 2004); available at:

www.haygroup.co.uk/downloads/The_Extended_School_report.pdf (accessed 17 May 2005).

37   S Johnson, 'Operators are standing by', *Wired Magazine* (November 2004); available at: www.wired.com/wired/archive/12.11/start.html?pg=2 (accessed 17 May 2005).

38   The Electoral Commission, *The European Parliamentary Elections in the United Kingdom* (London: The Electoral Commission, 2004).

39   M Weaver, 'Housing ballots prove more popular than the election', *Guardian*, 12 June 2001; see:
      http://society.guardian.co.uk/housingtransfers/story/0,8150,505620,00.html (accessed 17 May 2005).

40   M Sherraden, in W Paxton (ed), *Equal Shares? Building a progressive and coherent asset-based welfare policy* (London: ippr, 2003).

41   Craig. *Schools Out.*

42   See in particular the work of Manchester Community Pride in Manchester and Salford; see www.communitypride.org.uk (accessed 17 May 2005).

43   The Electoral Commission/The Hansard Society, *An Audit of Political Engagement* (London: The Electoral Commission/The Hansard Society, 2004).

44   T Bentley and P Miller, 'Party poopers', in *Financial Times Saturday Magazine*, 25 Sept 2004.

45   New Opportunities Fund and Community Fund, *Intelligent Funder Report* (London: Big Lottery Fund, forthcoming).

DEMOS – Licence to Publish

THE WORK (AS DEFINED BELOW) IS PROVIDED UNDER THE TERMS OF THIS LICENCE ("LICENCE"). THE WORK IS PROTECTED BY COPYRIGHT AND/OR OTHER APPLICABLE LAW. ANY USE OF THE WORK OTHER THAN AS AUTHORIZED UNDER THIS LICENCE IS PROHIBITED. BY EXERCISING ANY RIGHTS TO THE WORK PROVIDED HERE, YOU ACCEPT AND AGREE TO BE BOUND BY THE TERMS OF THIS LICENCE. DEMOS GRANTS YOU THE RIGHTS CONTAINED HERE IN CONSIDERATION OF YOUR ACCEPTANCE OF SUCH TERMS AND CONDITIONS.

1. **Definitions**
   a **"Collective Work"** means a work, such as a periodical issue, anthology or encyclopedia, in which the Work in its entirety in unmodified form, along with a number of other contributions, constituting separate and independent works in themselves, are assembled into a collective whole. A work that constitutes a Collective Work will not be considered a Derivative Work (as defined below) for the purposes of this Licence.
   b **"Derivative Work"** means a work based upon the Work or upon the Work and other pre-existing works, such as a musical arrangement, dramatization, fictionalization, motion picture version, sound recording, art reproduction, abridgment, condensation, or any other form in which the Work may be recast, transformed, or adapted, except that a work that constitutes a Collective Work or a translation from English into another language will not be considered a Derivative Work for the purpose of this Licence.
   c **"Licensor"** means the individual or entity that offers the Work under the terms of this Licence.
   d **"Original Author"** means the individual or entity who created the Work.
   e **"Work"** means the copyrightable work of authorship offered under the terms of this Licence.
   f **"You"** means an individual or entity exercising rights under this Licence who has not previously violated the terms of this Licence with respect to the Work, or who has received express permission from DEMOS to exercise rights under this Licence despite a previous violation.
2. **Fair Use Rights.** Nothing in this licence is intended to reduce, limit, or restrict any rights arising from fair use, first sale or other limitations on the exclusive rights of the copyright owner under copyright law or other applicable laws.
3. **Licence Grant.** Subject to the terms and conditions of this Licence, Licensor hereby grants You a worldwide, royalty-free, non-exclusive, perpetual (for the duration of the applicable copyright) licence to exercise the rights in the Work as stated below:
   a to reproduce the Work, to incorporate the Work into one or more Collective Works, and to reproduce the Work as incorporated in the Collective Works;
   b to distribute copies or phonorecords of, display publicly, perform publicly, and perform publicly by means of a digital audio transmission the Work including as incorporated in Collective Works;
   The above rights may be exercised in all media and formats whether now known or hereafter devised. The above rights include the right to make such modifications as are technically necessary to exercise the rights in other media and formats. All rights not expressly granted by Licensor are hereby reserved.
4. **Restrictions.** The licence granted in Section 3 above is expressly made subject to and limited by the following restrictions:
   a You may distribute, publicly display, publicly perform, or publicly digitally perform the work only under the terms of this Licence, and You must include a copy of, or the Uniform Resource Identifier for, this Licence with every copy or phonorecord of the Work You distribute, publicly display, publicly perform, or publicly digitally perform. You may not offer or impose any terms on the Work that alter or restrict the terms of this Licence or the recipients' exercise of the rights granted hereunder. You may not sublicence the Work. You must keep intact all notices that refer to this Licence and to the disclaimer of warranties. You may not distribute, publicly display, publicly perform, or publicly digitally perform the Work with any technological measures that control access or use of the Work in a manner inconsistent with the terms of this Licence Agreement. The above applies to the Work as incorporated in a Collective Work, but this does not require the Collective Work apart from the Work itself to be made subject to the terms of this Licence. If You create a Collective Work, upon notice from any Licencor You must, to the extent practicable, remove from the Collective Work any reference to such Licensor or the Original Author, as requested.
   b You may not exercise any of the rights granted to You in Section 3 above in any manner that is primarily intended for or directed toward commercial advantage or private monetary

compensation. The exchange of the Work for other copyrighted works by means of digital file-sharing or otherwise shall not be considered to be intended for or directed toward commercial advantage or private monetary compensation, provided there is no payment of any monetary compensation in connection with the exchange of copyrighted works.

c If you distribute, publicly display, publicly perform, or publicly digitally perform the Work or any Collective Works, You must keep intact all copyright notices for the Work and give the Original Author credit reasonable to the medium or means You are utilizing by conveying the name (or pseudonym if applicable) of the Original Author if supplied; the title of the Work if supplied. Such credit may be implemented in any reasonable manner; provided, however, that in the case of a Collective Work, at a minimum such credit will appear where any other comparable authorship credit appears and in a manner at least as prominent as such other comparable authorship credit.

5. Representations, Warranties and Disclaimer
   a By offering the Work for public release under this Licence, Licensor represents and warrants that, to the best of Licensor's knowledge after reasonable inquiry:
      i Licensor has secured all rights in the Work necessary to grant the licence rights hereunder and to permit the lawful exercise of the rights granted hereunder without You having any obligation to pay any royalties, compulsory licence fees, residuals or any other payments;
      ii The Work does not infringe the copyright, trademark, publicity rights, common law rights or any other right of any third party or constitute defamation, invasion of privacy or other tortious injury to any third party.
   b EXCEPT AS EXPRESSLY STATED IN THIS LICENCE OR OTHERWISE AGREED IN WRITING OR REQUIRED BY APPLICABLE LAW, THE WORK IS LICENCED ON AN "AS IS" BASIS, WITHOUT WARRANTIES OF ANY KIND, EITHER EXPRESS OR IMPLIED INCLUDING, WITHOUT LIMITATION, ANY WARRANTIES REGARDING THE CONTENTS OR ACCURACY OF THE WORK.

6. Limitation on Liability. EXCEPT TO THE EXTENT REQUIRED BY APPLICABLE LAW, AND EXCEPT FOR DAMAGES ARISING FROM LIABILITY TO A THIRD PARTY RESULTING FROM BREACH OF THE WARRANTIES IN SECTION 5, IN NO EVENT WILL LICENSOR BE LIABLE TO YOU ON ANY LEGAL THEORY FOR ANY SPECIAL, INCIDENTAL, CONSEQUENTIAL, PUNITIVE OR EXEMPLARY DAMAGES ARISING OUT OF THIS LICENCE OR THE USE OF THE WORK, EVEN IF LICENSOR HAS BEEN ADVISED OF THE POSSIBILITY OF SUCH DAMAGES.

7. Termination
   a This Licence and the rights granted hereunder will terminate automatically upon any breach by You of the terms of this Licence. Individuals or entities who have received Collective Works from You under this Licence, however, will not have their licences terminated provided such individuals or entities remain in full compliance with those licences. Sections 1, 2, 5, 6, 7, and 8 will survive any termination of this Licence.
   b Subject to the above terms and conditions, the licence granted here is perpetual (for the duration of the applicable copyright in the Work). Notwithstanding the above, Licensor reserves the right to release the Work under different licence terms or to stop distributing the Work at any time; provided, however that any such election will not serve to withdraw this Licence (or any other licence that has been, or is required to be, granted under the terms of this Licence), and this Licence will continue in full force and effect unless terminated as stated above.

8. Miscellaneous
   a Each time You distribute or publicly digitally perform the Work or a Collective Work, DEMOS offers to the recipient a licence to the Work on the same terms and conditions as the licence granted to You under this Licence.
   b If any provision of this Licence is invalid or unenforceable under applicable law, it shall not affect the validity or enforceability of the remainder of the terms of this Licence, and without further action by the parties to this agreement, such provision shall be reformed to the minimum extent necessary to make such provision valid and enforceable.
   c No term or provision of this Licence shall be deemed waived and no breach consented to unless such waiver or consent shall be in writing and signed by the party to be charged with such waiver or consent.
   d This Licence constitutes the entire agreement between the parties with respect to the Work licensed here. There are no understandings, agreements or representations with respect to the Work not specified here. Licensor shall not be bound by any additional provisions that may appear in any communication from You. This Licence may not be modified without the mutual written agreement of DEMOS and You.